THE MEDITERRANEAN DIET COOKBOOK FOR BEGINNERS.

125+ EASY, BOLD AND POCKET FRIENDLY FLAVORFUL RECIPES FOR HEALTHY LIVING. 30 MINUTES RECIPES. FULL COLOUR KITCHEN TESTED RECIPES FOR EVERYDAY LIVING

ROLL ALEX

ALEX PUBLISHING HOUSE

Copyright © OCTOBER 2024 ROLL ALEX

All rights reserved

The characters and events portrayed in this book are fictitious. Any similarity to real persons, living or dead, is coincidental and not intended by the author.

No part of this book may be reproduced, or stored in a retrieval system, or transmitted in any form or by any means, electronic, mechanical, photocopying, recording, or otherwise, without express written permission of the publisher.

9798344723594

Cover design by: Art Painter
Library of Congress Control Number: 2018675309
Printed in the United States of America

CONTENTS

Title Page
Copyright
CHAPTER 1   1
CHAPTER 2:   18
CHAPTER 3   36
CHAPTER 4   39
CHAPTER 5:   67
CHAPTER 6:   90
CHAPTER 7:   107
CHAPTER 8:   126
    149
CHAPTER 9:
    168
CHAPTER 10:
CHAPTER 11:   178
CHAPTER 12:   195
CHAPTER 13:   245
CHAPTER 14:   250

CHAPTER 1

Breakfast & Brunch

Shakshuka

Shakshuka is a spicy, full-bodied meal from North Africa that is popular throughout the Mediterranean. It is a colourful combination of poached eggs in a sauce made with pepper and tomatoes. It is typically eaten for brunch or breakfast, but it is becoming more and more well-liked as a filling dinner at any time of day. Shakshuka, with its harmony of crisp veggies, flavourful spices, and high-protein eggs, perfectly captures the spirit of Mediterranean cooking: it's straightforward, nourishing, and bursting with flavour.

Eggs are poached in a tomato-olive-olive oil sauce together with peppers, onions, garlic, and spices including paprika, cumin, cayenne, and nutmeg. This meal is known as shish-shouka. For millennia, the meal has been a part of Mediterranean cultures.

Ingredients

1 tablespoon of olive oil

1 sliced onion

2 minced cloves of garlic

1 chopped red pepper, one chopped green pepper, and one can (28 ounces/794 grams) chopped, undrained tomatoes

1 spoonful of pasted tomatoes

1 teaspoon of cumin powder

1/2 teaspoon of paprika

1/4 teaspoon black pepper and 1/2 teaspoon salt

6 big eggs

30 grams, or 1/4 cup Feta or goat cheese crumbles (optional)

Fresh cilantro or parsley chopped for garnish (optional)

Instruction:

1. In a big skillet, warm the olive oil over medium heat.
2. When the onion is soft and the garlic is aromatic, add the two and sauté for five to seven minutes.
3. When the peppers are soft, add the red and green bell peppers and sauté for 5 to 7 minutes.
4. In the skillet, add the diced tomatoes, tomato paste, cumin, paprika, salt, and black pepper. Stir to mix.
5. After lowering the heat to low, simmer the mixture

for ten to fifteen minutes, or until it begins to thicken somewhat.
6. Evenly divide the cracked eggs into the skillet.
7. When the whites of the eggs are set but the yolks are still runny, cover the skillet and cook the eggs for five to seven minutes.

Per-serving Nutritional Information:

300 calories

14g of protein

18g of fat

20g of carbohydrates

4g of fiber

The Turkish dish

This Turkish dish, called Çılbır (pronoun chil-bir), is essentially poached eggs served over a bed of thick, garlicky yogurt. It is garnished with a hefty pinch of Aleppo pepper (or equivalent red pepper flakes) and a liberal drizzle of heated butter (or, in my case, a robust extra virgin olive oil).

The majority of people associate yogurt with breakfast with anything as sugary as a parfait garnished with a few tablespoons of granola or fruit. However, this savory yogurt breakfast from Turkey is worth trying if you're ready for something different

While yogurt and eggs may not seem like a combination made in heaven, in Turkey they are. The yogurt has just enough garlic to give it a little kick without being overbearing. It's thick, chilled, and slightly sour. It gives the warm, runny poached eggs this amazing contrast.

Next is the butter, but this isn't just any butter. It's melted till boiling and combined with a small amount of Aleppo pepper or paprika. The butter acquires a rich, dark hue and a mild spiciness that harmonizes perfectly with the yogurt and eggs. It really brings the dish to life when you drizzle it over it. The smoothness of the yogurt, the spice from the pepper, and the butter's richness

In 2006, Çılbır and I initially met in Izmir, Turkey. The simplicity

of this incredibly rich poached egg breakfast surprised me! For such a simple recipe consisting of a few staples – eggs, yogurt, garlic, olive oil (or butter) – this savory Mediterranean breakfast is delicious and soothing in the nicest manner.

The finest way to finish off the last bit of thick, creamy yogurt on these Turkish eggs is to serve them right away with crusty country bread!

The highlight of this Turkish egg breakfast is the poached eggs, so make sure to poach them just right so you have nice, runny yolks covered in firm whites.

Ingredients

1 cup of Greek or coconut yogurt, plain

1 grated garlic clove

To taste, add salt and pepper.

1/2 a lemon, squeezed

2 tsp finely chopped parsley

Aleppo Butter:

1/4 cup of butter

1 tablespoon of Aleppo chili

1/2 a teaspoon of cumin

A half-tsp of paprika smoked

Eggs that have been stolen:

two eggs

choice of minced herbs (such chives, parsley, or cilantro) for garnish

Cherry Tomato Omelet

The Cherry Tomato Omelet is the ideal illustration of how a few fresh ingredients can improve a basic dish. It's really flavourful and quick to prepare, which makes it a great option for breakfast, brunch, or even a light dinner. The creamy smoothness of the eggs and the sweetness of the cherry tomatoes combine to create a dish that is both light and filling.

The tomatoes in this omelette are exceptionally fresh, which sets it apart. Just-cooked potatoes release their juices, which combine with the eggs to give each bite small flavor explosions. It's also really simple: just cut the tomatoes in half and gently sauté them before adding the eggs. You can add some extra depth by adding some sautéed onions or garlic, cheese, or even a handful of fresh herbs like parsley or basil. You can also keep it simple like that.

A cherry tomato omelette's adaptability is what makes it so beautiful. Do you want to keep it casual? Just add the eggs, tomatoes, and a dash of salt and pepper. Are you in the mood for something heartier? Add some spinach, feta or goat cheese crumbles, and possibly a few olives. It can be customized according to your mood or the ingredients you happen to have on hand.

It's easy to make a cherry tomato omelette by heating up some olive oil in a skillet, sautéing the tomatoes until they start to soften, and then adding the whisked eggs. Cook the omelette gently until it sets, then fold it over and serve. Even on the busiest mornings, you can still feel as like you've created something special when you serve this kind of breakfast.

Ingredients

1 cup of egg whites

1/2 a dozen cherry tomatoes

1 cup of baby spinach

To season, add salt and pepper.

Instructions

Beat egg whites together and transfer to a medium-high heat nonstick skillet.

Evenly top the egg whites with the tomatoes and spinach.

Give the egg whites five to eight minutes to fully set.

Flip the sides of the egg white into an omelette and place it on a platter using a big spatula.

The Herby Mushroom Frittata

The Herby Mushroom Frittata is an ideal option if you're searching for a dish that's earthy and fresh at the same time. Light, fluffy eggs bind together a fragrant blend of herbs and the rich, savory flavor of mushrooms in this Mediterranean-inspired frittata. It is the kind of dish that is perfect for breakfast, brunch, or even a quick dinner because it feels decadent but still healthful.
In a big skillet over low heat, melt the butter.

This herbaceous mushroom frittata's adaptability is what makes it so wonderful. It can be as basic or as complex as you like. For a crisp, fresh taste, stick to only mushrooms and herbs. Alternatively, add some caramelized onions for sweetness, a handful of spinach, or a sprinkle of cheese (feta or goat cheese). Adapting it to what you have on hand is simple.

The frittata is really easy to make. The first step is to sauté the mushrooms until they are soft and brown. After that, top with the whisked eggs and garnish with your fresh herbs. The secret to a fantastic frittata is to cook it slowly, starting on the burner and working your way up to the oven until it's cooked through without drying out. The end product is a frittata that has a creamy, velvety interior and a golden outside.

The finest aspect? This frittata is ideal for preparing meals. It's something you can prepare in advance, cut into wedges, and eat all week. It's a satisfying and easy

choice for both casual dining and on-the-go eating because it tastes great both warm and cold.

The next time you're in the mood for something hearty and flavourful, try this herbaceous mushroom frittata. It's an easy recipe to prepare, but it tastes great and leaves you feeling full!

Instruction.

After adding, simmer the sliced mushrooms for a few minutes.

Transfer the eggs into a bowl and use a fork to gently whisk them.

For the eggs, grind some black pepper.

To the mushrooms, add the eggs. To cover the pan's base, swirl around.

When the egg is fully cooked, add the herbs and simmer over low heat.

You might finish in the grill to fully cook the top of the egg.

overnight oats

Overnight Oats are as its name suggests soaked at night with either milk/curd. And served as breakfast with fruits/nuts/honey added to it, for additional taste.Preferably served cold, as its refrigerated.
When you have a hectic morning and want something quick, easy, and nutritious, overnight oats are the ideal answer. You make this easy, no-cook breakfast the night before, and when you wake up, a creamy, delectable meal is ready for you. The wonderful thing about overnight oats is their versatility; you can add any number of flavors to keep things interesting.

The foundation is simple: rolled oats soaked in a liquid (often milk or a dairy-free substitute, such as oat or almond milk). The liquid is absorbed by the oats while they sit overnight, giving them a creamy, delicious, and easily digestible texture. You can add chia seeds to add a little nutritional boost, or yogurt for added creaminess and protein.

However, adding mix-ins is where the real excitement lies. Nuts, seeds, fresh or dried fruits, and spices turn plain oats into a tasty, well-balanced breakfast. Try adding banana slices, a little honey, and a dash of cinnamon for a simple and sweet treat. If you're in the mood for something a little richer, add some chopped almonds, chocolate nibs, and peanut butter. You can even try making savory variations with additions of herbs, avocado, and a small amount of olive oil.

Overnight oats are nutrient-dense in addition to being handy. Aside from providing vitamins, antioxidants, and healthy fats, mix-ins like fruits and nuts also add fiber, which helps keep you full throughout the morning. You may feed your day without having to rely on processed or sugary meals with this ideal method.

It's quite simple to make overnight oats. Everything is simply combined in a basin or jar, refrigerated, and left to work over time. You may eat them cold out of the refrigerator in the morning, or simply reheat them in the microwave if you'd rather have something warmer.

The finest aspect? You may quickly prepare multiple jars in advance, providing you with breakfast for the next few days. The flexibility and nutrients that overnight oats provide can help you tackle any kind of morning, be it leisurely or hectic.

Ingredients

½ cup of traditional oats

½ cup milk (use whatever kind you choose)

1 tsp of unadulterated maple syrup

1 tsp of pure vanilla essence and any desired toppings, such as granola, bananas, strawberries, or blueberries

Put everything into a mason jar. Cover and shake to combine. (If preparing a bigger quantity, you can mix the components in a bowl.)

For at least six hours and up to three days, refrigerate. Top with chosen toppings and serve.

THE MEDITERRANEAN DIET COOKBOOK FOR BEGINNERS

CHAPTER 2:

Juices, Shakes & Smoothies

Orange, Ginger, and Mint juice

The delicious and energizing combination of orange, ginger, and mint juice has the ideal ratio of sweetness, zest, and spice. It's more than simply a beverage; it's a health-conscious energy enhancer that can revitalize you whenever you need it or help you start your day.

Fresh oranges provide the juice's natural sweetness and zesty foundation. Vitamin C, an antioxidant found in abundance in oranges, boosts your immune system, encourages good skin, and helps you feel invigorated. Plus, oranges are a really refreshing fruit, especially when combined with the strong flavors of ginger and mint.

Ginger gives the juice a really nice spicy kick. Ginger not only adds warmth to the mixture but is also well-known for its ability to help with digestion and reduce inflammation. A tiny quantity can improve circulation, ease upset stomachs, and even lessen tired muscles after exercise. It's one of those foods that tastes amazing and has amazing health benefits.

Then there's the fragrant, vibrant, and fresh mint. The sweetness of the orange and the spice of the ginger are cooled by the mint leaves. They provide taste and functionality to this beverage, as well as aiding with digestion and breath freshening.

The best thing about this juice is how simple it is to prepare. Just squeeze in some fresh orange juice, stir in some torn mint leaves, and add a small amount of grated ginger (you don't need much!). The juice can be left pulpy for a more rustic look, or strained for a smoother texture. Though the natural sweetness of the oranges is typically more than sufficient, a little drizzle of honey or agave can pull everything together if you want an extra bit of sweetness.

This mixture is a fantastic way to get a vitamin and nutrition boost while staying hydrated. It's great for breakfast, as a post-workout beverage, or as a cool treat on a hot day. For added cooling, you might also serve it cold with ice.

This juice is a powerhouse of wellbeing in a glass, combining immune-boosting oranges, ginger that's good for digestion, and cooling mint. For anybody seeking a bright and reviving beverage, Orange, Ginger, and Mint Juice is a go-to option because it's easy to make, packed with health benefits, and flavourful.

Kefir Banana Shake with Fresh Berries

Although it's usually ideal to consume whole fruit, smoothies are a terrific, quick way to get a lot of fruit (or veggies) in one cup. This smoothie contains kefir, which is rich in probiotic cultures and helps maintain a healthy gut.

This is a different take on our recipe for the kefir smoothie base.

Smoothies made with kefir are an excellent way to start the day, get you through a workout, or just to quench your want for something cool, creamy, and sweet! This smoothie with banana, berries, and kefir is incredibly tasty, simple to prepare, and full of nutritious components

Sweet bananas, vivid fresh berries, and creamy kefir come together in the delectable and nutrient-rich Kefir Banana Shake with Fresh Berries. This shake is a great addition to your daily routine because it's not just a refreshing delight but also a probiotic, vitamin, and antioxidant powerhouse.

Kefir, a fermented dairy product with a thinner, more palatable consistency than yogurt, serves as the foundation of this shake. Probiotics are the "good" bacteria found in kefir that help with digestion, immune system stimulation, and gut health. With a creamy, tangy base that goes well with fruit, it's a terrific method to nourish your digestive system.

Bananas give the shake its inherent sweetness and creaminess. Rich in potassium and fiber, they contribute to electrolyte balance, long-lasting energy, and a velvety texture that elevates the shake to a decadent level. Additionally, bananas work wonders with kefir, reducing its acidity and producing a well-balanced, mellow flavor.

Whether you use blueberries, raspberries, strawberries, or a combination, the fresh berries add a plethora of antioxidants and a vibrant pop of color. Berries are well-known for their abundance in vitamin C and other nutrients that promote healthy skin, strengthen the immune system, and reduce inflammation. In order to create a harmonious flavor profile, they also add a hint of acidity that balances the sweetness of the banana and the tang of the kefir.

The shake is quite easy to make. Simply process a ripe banana, a few of your preferred fresh berries, and kefir until a smooth consistency is achieved. If you want a thinner shake, add more kefir; if you want a frostier texture, add extra ice. To enhance the nutritional value even more, you may wish to use a small amount of protein powder, flaxseeds, or chia seeds.

You can have this Kefir Banana Shake with Fresh Berries for breakfast, as a light dessert, or even as a post-workout snack. It is naturally sweet, full of fiber and protein, and has no artificial sweeteners or additives, making it satiating and invigorating.

Ingredients

Banana: Swap it out for another creamy fruit, like avocados or mangos.

Berries: any frozen fruit will do.

Kefir: use 1/2 cup plain Greek yogurt or ordinary yogurt plus 1/2 cup non dairy milk.

Replace kale for spinach, but be aware that the taste is a little different. Never use mustard greens or arugula. Bananas are a great way to mask the flavor of leafy greens in smoothies if you're not sure how your smoothie will taste with greens in it.

This smoothie fulfills your needs for a quick, wholesome breakfast on the road or for replenishing your body after working out. It's creamy, fruity, and packed with nutrients that sustain life in every sip—the ideal combination of flavor and health benefits.

Pineapple Mint Shake

I'm going back to one of our best-loved, kid-friendly pineapple smoothie recipes from Milo's preschool days today: pineapple mint smoothies!

This vibrant, fresh pineapple mint smoothie is a tasty combination of flavors that includes a good amount of greens. It may readily absorb additional smoothie boosters to increase the amount of nutrients in the smoothie. It's a quick and simple nutritious breakfast or afternoon snack that's light and satisfying.

A crisp, energizing freshness of mint combined with the sweet, acidic flavor of ripe pineapple creates a delightfully refreshing tropical treat known as the Pineapple Mint Shake. This shake is a favorite for hot days, post-workout treats, or anytime you need something light and energizing since it's the ideal balance of flavor and hydration.

The star of the shake, the pineapple, is not only delicious but also nutrient-dense. Pineapple aids with digestion, immunity, and skin health. It is high in vitamin C, manganese, and the digestive enzyme bromelain. Because of its inherent sweetness, this smoothie doesn't require additional sugar, making it a pleasant and health-conscious option.

On the other hand, mint gives the tropical flavor a cool edge. The luscious sweetness of pineapple and the freshness of mint combine to create a balance that is both comforting and invigorating. This smoothie is not only delicious but also beneficial due to the digestive benefits of mint, which include its ability to calm the stomach and freshen breath.

The simplicity of the Pineapple Mint Shake is what really sets it apart. Only a few fresh or frozen pineapple chunks, a few fresh mint leaves, and a liquid base are needed to make it. For something creamier and more nutrient-dense, try coconut water, almond milk, or yogurt instead of just water. Everything should be blended until smooth to create a colourful, nutrient-rich smoothie.

In addition to being delicious, the Pineapple Mint Shake is hydrating and full of vitamins, antioxidants, and digestive support. Enjoy this smoothie as a midday snack, post-workout hydrator, or morning pick-me-up; it has a refreshing burst of tropical flavor with a minty finish. Your body and taste buds will appreciate this refreshing, healthful, and light beverage.

So, try this Pineapple Mint Shake the next time you're craving something fruity and fresh. It's the ideal method to replenish your energy and nourishment in one delectable glass.

ROLL ALEX

Ingredients

What Makes a Mint Smoothie?

To make this delectable mint smoothie, head to the grocery store and pick up the following fruits, leafy greens, and fresh herbs.

A juicy, sweet pineapple smoothie tastes great served anyplace. It's the ideal summertime beverage to stay hydrated, feel great, and cool down!

Kale: The queen of the leafy greens, kale is a great source of fiber and phytonutrients that are beneficial to our health.

The most hydrating liquid foundation available is coconut water. On hot days or as a smoothie after working out, I adore consuming it.

Pineapple: This fruity smoothie becomes a luscious poolside treat thanks to the natural sweetness.

Lime: When combined into a mint smoothie, fresh limes create the most brilliant flavors.

Mint: A natural stimulant, mint can help you get motivated before hitting the gym or even during one of those excruciatingly dull afternoons.

Chocolate Peanut Protein Smoothie

With a rich, creamy flavor that satisfies your sweet craving and provides your body with vital nutrients, the Chocolate Peanut Protein Smoothie is the perfect blend of indulgence and nutrition. Rich in protein, healthy fats, and energetic ingredients, this makes it a great choice for breakfast, a lunchtime snack, or recovery after a workout.

This smoothie's base is the age-old pairing of chocolate and peanut butter, which is incredibly irresistible. The fundamental flavor of chocolate is provided by the rich, velvety taste of cocoa, which adds a sumptuous flavor without the guilt. This smoothie is a multifaceted treat that boosts heart health and elevates mood thanks to the abundance of antioxidants found in cocoa.

Beyond adding a nutty flavor, peanut butter is an excellent source of protein, fiber, and healthy fats. Together, these nutrients help you feel satisfied and invigorated all day long. Furthermore, peanut butter has essential vitamins and minerals like potassium and magnesium that promote overall health and muscle function.

You can add a scoop of your preferred protein powder to increase the protein amount. This inclusion, which can be plant-based, whey, or collagen protein, aids in muscle regeneration and encourages recovery following exercise, which makes the Chocolate Peanut Protein Smoothie a great choice for after a workout. Protein is a fantastic way to refuel because it promotes metabolism and helps rebuild muscles.

The inherent sweetness and creaminess of bananas, together with their smooth texture and potassium content, make them a popular addition. Potassium helps maintain fluid balance and stave off muscular cramps. If you would rather have something lower in carbohydrates, you may replace the banana with an avocado, which offers a surge of beneficial fats and creaminess without adding any sugar.

You may use almond milk, coconut milk, or even ordinary milk for extra creaminess when blending it all together. For an even more delicious smoothie, you may add additional ice to give it a chilly, foamy texture.

The Chocolate Peanut Protein Smoothie's delectable texture belies its nutritional value, which supports your body's optimal function and well-being. It's rich but healthy, filling but not overindulgent.

The Chocolate Peanut Protein Smoothie is the perfect solution if you're wanting to replenish your energy after working out, need a quick breakfast on the run, or just want a tasty snack that's also packed with nutrients. You may feel good about indulging in this blend of flavors and benefits at any time of day.

How to Prepare a Protein Shake with Chocolate and Peanut Butter:

1. Make Sure Your Milk Is Cold

You can buy some plant-based milks in aseptic, non-refrigerated containers. Before using an unopened container in this recipe, we advise putting it in the refrigerator. It will guarantee that your smoothie turns out cold and creamy!

2. Employ a Completely Ripe Banana

Make sure you wait until your banana peel is mottled brown and dark yellow for a naturally sweet smoothie. Cut into slices, put them in a freezer bag, and freeze. Don't add the slices to the smoothie until they are completely frozen. See the section below for more thorough information on freezing bananas.

3. Select powdered unsweetened cocoa.

Although most cocoa powders are unsweetened, it's a good idea to double-check the labels. Make sure you double-check the packaging for cocoa powder and hot cocoa mix, as they sometimes share shelf space.

4. Mix It Up!

One serving of this smoothie recipe yields roughly two cups. You can use a standard blender or a smaller, personal-size blender. Both function quite well. You can double the recipe if you are serving more people!

Spinach, Cucumber, Celery,

and Apple Juice

With every sip, the nutrient-dense blend of spinach, cucumber, celery, and apple juice gives you a vitamin and hydration boost. This juice is ideal for a mid-afternoon pick-me-up or a refreshing morning drink since it mixes the natural sweetness of apple with the crispness of cucumber and celery with the earthy goodness of spinach.

Iron, calcium, and vitamin K are all abundant in spinach, a nutrient-dense food that is crucial for good bones, blood, and general health. Additionally, it has a lot of antioxidants, which support healthy skin and reduce inflammation. An easy method to get these nutrients without the bulk of a salad is to blend spinach into a juice.

Cucumber gives the drink a cool, moisturizing touch. Cucumber makes you feel light and rejuvenated by flushing out toxins thanks to its high water content and low calorie level. Additionally, it is a natural source of vitamins K and C, which help maintain healthy bones and an immune system.

Celery is another important ingredient in this mixture because of its reputation for detoxification. It is excellent for digestion because it is low in calories and high in fiber. In addition to its potential to lower inflammation and promote heart health, celery also has other chemicals that enhance the juice's crisp, clean flavor.

Everything is brought together by the sweetness of the apple, which counteracts the crispness of the cucumber and celery and the earthiness of the spinach. In addition to being delicious, apples are also a great source of fiber and vitamin C, which help healthy digestion and strengthen the immune system. They naturally sweeten the juice, so there's no need for additional sweeteners, making it a healthy choice for people who prefer their food to be tasty but light.

Making the Spinach, Cucumber, Celery, and Apple Juice is quite easy. Simply process until smooth, adding diced cucumber, celery stalks, crisp apple, and fresh spinach leaves. Add a small amount of water or coconut water to make it thinner. Add some ice for a colder, refreshing beverage as well.

This juice is a great way to hydrate your body and provide it with a combination of vital nutrients, in addition to being delicious. It's ideal as a refreshing, nutrient-rich drink whenever you need a healthy boost, or as a burst of energy to start your day.

The Spinach, Cucumber, Celery, and Apple Juice is a great option whether you want to boost your intake of vegetables, improve your digestion, or just enjoy a delicious, fresh juice. It has the ideal ratio of flavor to health benefits. This green beverage is healthy for both your body and your palate.

Ingredients

1/2 cucumber, chopped and peeled

1/2 Red or green apple

1 celery stick

1 tablespoon of either lime or lemon juice, or to taste

Optional: a pinch of salt

Direction

Cut 1/2 of a cucumber into large pieces after peeling. Dice one celery stick and half an apple into large pieces. You can also peel the apple, if you'd like.

Put the apple, cucumber, and celery in a large blender jar. Add one tablespoon each of lemon or lime juice. Pour in half a cup of water.

Once the cover is closed, mix until smooth.

Place three to four ice cubes in a serving glass. Drizzle with the prepared juice and sprinkle with salt. Cucumber Apple It is time to serve the celery juice. Before serving, if desired, strain the juice through a fine-mesh strainer. Drink this juice right away to reap the greatest benefits. It can be refrigerated for up to one day.

CHAPTER 3

Meze, Antipasti, Tapas, and Other Small Plates

The core of Mediterranean cuisine is found in meze, antipasti, tapas, and other small plates. Here, meals are about more than just providing sustenance; they're also about sharing, mingling, and experiencing a range of flavors. These little plates are ideal for both informal and formal parties, as they provide an opportunity to sample a variety of ingredients, flavors, and textures all at once.

Meze

Meze is a Middle Eastern and Eastern Mediterranean ritual that consists of a variety of tiny, savory foods that are meant to go well together. These can be anything from marinated olives, stuffed grape leaves (dolma), and grilled halloumi cheese to creamy hummus, zesty tzatziki, and smoky baba ganoush. The balance of meze is what makes it so beautiful; each plate has a unique flavor that compliments the others, making for a varied and delicious meal experience.

Antipasti

Similar to this, antipasti, an Italian appetizer, usually features seasonal, fresh foods and acts as a preamble to the main course. Marinated veggies like peppers and artichokes, cured meats like salami and prosciutto, and cheeses like pecorino or mozzarella can all be served as antipasti. It's all about keeping things simple and highlighting the flavors of the ingredients, which are frequently seasoned with herbs and a dash of olive oil.

The customary first course of an Italian meal is called antipasto. Antipasti is served on a platter, usually in bite-sized little amounts for each person to help themselves from, with the aim of stimulating the appetite.

Tapas

On the Spanish side, tapas provide meals with a vibrant, communal element. Tapas can include heated appetizers like gambas al ajillo (garlic shrimp), chorizo al vino (chorizo in wine), and patatas bravas (fried potatoes with a spicy tomato sauce). Cold appetizers like olives, manchego cheese, and jamón ibérico can also be considered tapas. Tapas are typically served with beverages, but they're really meant to be shared. Each little bite-sized amount packs a flavourful punch, so feel free to mix and match and share with friends.

All of these traditions are united by their emphasis on high-quality ingredients, straightforward cooking, and the delight of sharing. These little dishes are perfect for sharing over drinks with friends, beginning an Italian meal with antipasti, or savoring a variety of meze on a sunny afternoon.

Since small plates frequently include a variety of veggies, grains, proteins, and healthy fats, including them in your eating routine is also a terrific way to enjoy a balanced meal. There are countless options for tasty, nutritious, and communal eating with Meze, Antipasti, Tapas, and Other Small Plates, whether you're throwing a party, having a laid-back lunch, or you just want to try something new.

CHAPTER 4

Salads

Cannellini Bean and Red Pepper Salad

A touch of lemon and roasted red peppers liven up this cannellini bean salad. This is the ideal light summer meal in my opinion; all I need is a slice of crusty bread to satisfy my hunger.

Every now and then you need a simple summer meal. To be honest, I could eat like this all day long. Just having a simple, light salad for dinner is one of my favorite dining experiences. A piece of toast to mop up all the yummy goodness that settles at the bottom of the salad bowl. Orange adds a lovely warm flavor to the dressing and enhances it. In order to accentuate the flavors, I have also added some lemon juice. I don't think orange can accomplish this task by itself.

Orange adds a lovely warm flavor to the dressing and enhances it. In order to accentuate the flavors, I have also added some lemon juice. I don't think orange can accomplish this task by itself.

A colourful and nutrient-dense dish, the Cannellini Bean and Red Pepper Salad combines healthful, fresh ingredients in a delicious combination of textures and flavors. It's the epitome of Mediterranean simplicity, where every component is given room to flourish and work together to create a well-rounded and filling meal.

Cannellini beans are the main ingredient in this salad; they're mild, creamy, and full of fiber and protein. This salad is not only tasty but also substantial and satisfying because of the white beans, which are a great source of plant-based protein. Their subtle flavor serves as the ideal counterpoint to the dish's other, more colourful elements.

The red bell peppers provide a delightful crunch, as well as a flash of color and sweetness. Red peppers, which are high in antioxidants and vitamin C, not only improve the taste of the salad but also have health advantages that boost the immune system and improve skin health. Every mouthful tastes good because of the way their crunchy texture contrasts with the soft beans.

A refreshing, aromatic touch is added by adding fresh herbs like parsley or basil to the salad, which balances the beans and peppers. Everything is brought together with a simple vinaigrette consisting of extra virgin olive oil, lemon juice, garlic, and maybe a hint of mustard. The lemon offers a zesty, bright zing that lifts the tastes, while the olive oil supplies heart-healthy fats.

Additional ingredients in some variations of this salad include cucumbers for crunch, red onions for a hint of sharpness, or even feta cheese for a contrast of salt and creaminess. It's a very flexible recipe that you can simply modify to suit your tastes or what you have on hand.

Cannellini bean and red pepper salad is a simple yet flavourful dish that strikes the perfect balance between hardiness and lightness. It's a nutrient-dense, tasty, and fast-to-prepare alternative that can be eaten as a side dish at supper or as the main portion of a light lunch.

This salad is ideal for meal prep or to take to parties since it can be prepared in advance, allowing the flavors to mingle. It's an excellent option for anyone who wants to increase the amount of plant-based foods in their diet without sacrificing flavor or satisfaction.

Ingredients

2 tablespoons of extra virgin olive oil

2 tablespoon of coarsely chopped capers from the zest of one orange and one orange juice from one lemon

I use low-sodium kinds of beans, about 1 can washed and drained, and 1 ½ cups cooked cannellini beans or white kidney beans.

3 to four entire roasted red peppers roughly one cup, sliced

¼ cup of freshly chopped herbs basil, parsley, and chives

½ cup tiny diced red onions

One minced garlic clove, salted to taste

Asparagus Pasta Salad

Asparagus Pasta Salad is a delicious combination of fresh, vibrant flavors and textures. This meal, which highlights the crisp, sensitive bite of asparagus with thick pasta, is perfect for spring or summer and is a healthful and adaptable choice for any occasion.

The main attraction in this salad is the asparagus. In addition to being high in antioxidants, fiber, and vitamins A, C, and K, this nutrient-dense vegetable has a delightfully mild, slightly sweet flavor. Asparagus retains its vibrant green hue and crisp-tender texture when it is gently cooked or blanched, which creates the ideal contrast with the pasta's tenderness.

Pasta serves as the main ingredient in the recipe, giving the salad body and a reassuring texture. Any kind of pasta will do, but small pasta shapes like fusilli, farfalle, or penne are especially useful because they absorb the dressing and combine with the other ingredients with ease. If you want to add extra nutrients to the salad, whole-grain or gluten-free alternatives are also great possibilities.

Many recipes add other fresh ingredients, such as cherry tomatoes for a juicy burst of sweetness, red onions for a little bite, and even olives or artichoke hearts for a Mediterranean flavor, to balance the asparagus and pasta. Herbs such as basil, parsley, or dill infuse the dish with a delicious freshness that makes it feel quite summery.

The lemon-ricotta dressing is what makes this asparagus pasta salad so delicious. This creamy sauce gives this cold pasta salad a pleasant boost of protein and a velvety texture, and it comes together in a matter of minutes.

Typically, the dressing consists of a zesty, light vinaigrette made with extra virgin olive oil, lemon juice, and maybe some garlic or Dijon mustard. The olive oil offers healthful fats and a smooth, silky texture that properly coats the pasta and vegetables, while the lemon gives an acidic brightness that goes well with the earthy asparagus. Grated Parmesan or crumbled feta, both of which lend a salty, creamy flavor that balances the salad's freshness, can be added for a deeper variation.

The variety of the asparagus pasta salad is what draws people in. It can be served cold as a cool side dish or cooked as a main course. Additionally, it's simple to alter—you can add grilled chicken, shrimp, or even

Why you will love it.

Easy and Quick: This pasta salad with lemon and asparagus takes only 20 minutes to prepare.

Creamy-A thick and creamy dressing made with ricotta cheese, olive oil, garlic, and lemon juice guarantees that every bite of this pasta salad is bursting with flavor.

Rich in Fiber: This pasta salad laden with vegetables is a tasty and healthful way to make sure you're eating your veggies and meeting your daily fiber requirements.

Keeps Well: This pasta salad makes excellent leftovers that you can eat for days on end or as a nice make-ahead meal. It keeps well in the refrigerator for up to five days.

Ingredients

Pasta: For this recipe, I suggest using short-cut pasta because its shape goes well with the asparagus. Although fusilli, penne, farfalle, cavatappi, gemelli, and cavatelli would all work well, I used rotini pasta in my recipes.

Asparagus The main ingredient in this recipe for creamy asparagus pasta salad is asparagus. Use fresh asparagus whenever possible; frozen asparagus should not be used as it will get soggy.

Radish: To add more veggies, color, crunch, and a bite of zest. Carrots and zucchini would be excellent substitutes if you're not a fan of radishes.

Green Peas: To provide extra fiber and a burst of freshness. Although fresh peas can be used instead of frozen ones in this dish, specific instructions are provided in the recipe card's notes section.

Fresh Herbs: To add some freshness and lush greens, combine fresh parsley and fresh dill. It would also be good with some fresh mint and basil.

Ricotta: To make the dressing rich and creamy and to give it an extra protein boost. Ricotta cheese can be made with whole or skim milk; alternatively, it can be made with cottage cheese, sour cream, or plain Greek yogurt.

Olive Oil: For the dressing preparation. I used extra virgin olive oil, but you may use any type of olive oil or even avocado oil.

Lemon: Used to make the creamy lemon ricotta dressing, lemon zest and juice are combined. If you don't have any fresh lemons, you can substitute red wine or lemon juice concentrate in place of the zest.

Instruction

1. Prepare the dressing. In a small jar or bowl, combine the ricotta cheese, olive oil, garlic, lemon juice, lemon zest, and salt; stir to mix while the pasta cooks.
2. Prepare the vegetables. Mince the dill and parsley, slice the radishes, then trim and chop the asparagus.
3. Cook the vegetables in boiling water. In a small pot of boiling water, add the asparagus and simmer for 2 minutes. Then, add the green peas and cook for 1 more minute. After cooking, place prepared food in a bowl of cold water to cool.
4. Bring the spaghetti to a boil. The uncooked pasta should be added to a large pot of boiling salted water and cooked until al dente, following the instructions on the package.
5. Pasta should be cooled. Once cooked, chill the pasta by straining it through a wide colander and running it under cold water.
6. Combine the pasta salad ingredients. In a big bowl, add the cooked pasta, asparagus, green peas, radish, parsley, and dill. Drizzle with the lemon-ricotta dressing and mix thoroughly. As necessary, taste and adjust the seasoning with more salt and pepper.
7. Present and savor! Serve the pasta salad with asparagus right away, or refrigerate it for up to five days in an airtight container.

Fattoush

A tasty and colourful salad from the Middle East, fattoush is known for its vibrancy. It's a celebration of crisp pita bread and seasonal, fresh veggies dressed with a spicy, tart sauce. This dish is a mainstay in many Mediterranean diets because of its robust flavors and ease of preparation.

Fresh vegetables including tomatoes, cucumbers, radishes, and leafy greens are the main ingredients of fattoush. These components give the salad a vibrant texture and balance because they offer the ideal amount of crunch, juiciness, and natural sweetness. Cucumbers and radishes add a crisp, cool bite, and tomatoes bring a surge of acidity. Fresh herbs like parsley or mint are frequently added to the mixture, which adds a fragrant and aromatic layer that brightens

Essentially a "bread salad," fattoush is a dish that originated in northern Lebanon. For added flavor, Lebanese farmers would fry their leftover pita scraps in a small amount of olive oil. They would also just toss the pita chips in with whatever seasonal veggies and herbs they happen to have on hand to construct their fattoush.

Fattoush is unique among salads because it includes crispy pita bread. Usually, leftover pita is broken up and mixed into the salad after being fried or roasted until golden and crisp. This gives the dish a distinct texture as each bite contrasts the luscious, fresh veggies with the delightful crunch of the pita. Additionally, the dressing flavors are absorbed by the pita, enhancing the flavor of each bite.

Usually created with freshly squeezed lemon juice, olive oil, and sumac—a sour, reddish spice that is a hallmark of Middle Eastern cuisine—the dressing for fattoush is a lemony vinaigrette. Sumac lifts the citrus notes and elegantly binds the vegetables together in the salad with its unique acidity and depth of taste. Pomegranate syrup, garlic, and a tiny teaspoon of salt.

One of the best things about **Fattoush** is its versatility. You can make it as light or hearty as you like by adjusting the ingredients —some variations include bell peppers, onions, or even grilled vegetables for added depth. The salad is naturally vegetarian and can easily be adapted to vegan diets, making it an accessible dish for a wide range of tastes and dietary preferences.

Fattoush is perfect as a side dish for grilled meats, kebabs, or falafel, but it's also hearty enough to stand on its own as a light, satisfying meal. Its bright, fresh flavors make it a great option for warm weather, picnics, or any time you want something refreshing and wholesome.

How to Prepare fattoush.

1. Begin by choosing the freshest produce you can find, such as ripe tomatoes and freshly harvested herbs.
2. Store-bought pita chips are not recommended; while they have their place, it's not in fattoush salad. Make sure to season your pita properly when toasting and frying them at home.
3. Do your best not to skip sumac. The acidic flavor of this unique spice, which is made from pulverized sumac berries, is extremely difficult to duplicate.
4. Make use of the finest extra virgin olive oil available. Its fruity, peppery flavor is crucial in this situation. Recall that olive oils with the term "pure" on them have typically undergone mechanical refining and heat treatment, leaving them flavorless and lacking in character.
5. Finally, keep in mind that this is a "basic" fattoush recipe. Feel free to create your own version by incorporating seasonal veggies such as vibrant heirloom tomatoes or even green peppers. Add smashed garlic or other herbs. Additionally, add one teaspoon of pomegranate molasses to the vinaigrette, if you have access to it.

Ingredients

2 pita bread loaves

Extra virgin olive oil

salt that is kosher

Split 2 tsp sumac; add more as necessary

1 sliced Romaine lettuce heart

1 English cucumber, sliced or chopped into half-moon shapes after the seeds are removed.

5 Roma tomatoes, cut Five green onions, chopped, both the green and white sections

Cut 5 radishes thinly after removing the stems.

2 cups of finely cut, fresh parsley leaves without stems

1 cup of freshly chopped mint leaves (optional)

Panzanella

A typical summertime dish in Tuscany, panzanella, also known as panmolle, is a chopped salad of soaked stale bread, onions, and tomatoes. It is topped with vinegar and olive oil and frequently contains cucumbers and basil. In other areas of central Italy, it is also well-liked.

A classic Tuscan bread salad, panzanella takes basic ingredients and creates a dish that is full of texture and taste. It's a wonderful illustration of traditional Italian cookery, in which nothing is wasted, even day-old bread. Juicy tomatoes, crisp cucumbers, aromatic basil, and, of course, slices of bread that absorb all the wonderful dressing flavors make up the ideal salad combo.

The bread is the main ingredient in panzanella. Usually, old or leftover crusty bread, like rustic Italian loaf, is utilized. To ensure that the bread absorbs the juices from the veggies and dressing without being too soggy, it is either lightly toasted or soaked in cubes. The goal is for the bread to absorb the flavors like a sponge while retaining some texture.

Another important component that gives the salad a boost of freshness and juiciness is the tomatoes. For optimal flavor, use ripe, in-season tomatoes (heirloom or vine-ripened kinds are great). Their naturally occurring juices blend well with the dressing to produce a bright, summery flavor, and they provide a sweet and tangy balance to the hefty bread.

Red onions offer a mild sharpness that balances well with the sweetness of the tomatoes, while cucumbers lend a cool crunch. Fresh basil is crucial since it gives the salad a wonderful scent that melds well with the other components.

A simple yet flavourful dressing consisting of extra virgin olive oil, red wine vinegar, salt, and pepper is typically used for panzanella. Richness is added by the olive oil, and the dish is brought together by the tangy acidity of the vinegar. For an additional flavor boost, several recipes may use a dash of garlic or capers.

The versatility of panzanella is one of its best features. To add extra depth and a briny taste, you can add grilled veggies like bell peppers or zucchini, or you can add mozzarella for a creamy texture. This recipe is quite adaptable and goes well as an accompaniment to grilled meats or seafood. However, it can also be a filling and light supper on its own, especially in the summer.

Recipe

Slice the bread into rounds approximately 1 cm thick for the traditional panzanella recipe, then lay them out flat in a sizable ovenproof dish. After lightly pressing them with your hands to saturate them, wet them with 250 g of water and leave them to rest for 40–45 minutes.

Ingredients

Four servings

500g of ripe, firm tomatoes

400 grams of old Tuscan bread

One red onion

One cucumber

fifteen basil leaves

Six fillets of anchovies

Ten capers

vinegar made from white wine

extra virgin olive oil

salt

chili

Instruction

First Step

Slice the bread into rounds approximately 1 cm thick for the traditional panzanella recipe, then lay them out flat in a sizable ovenproof dish. After lightly pressing them with your hands to saturate them, wet them with 250 g of water and leave them to rest for 40–45 minutes.

Step Two

After peeling and slicing the onion, combine it with 70 g of water and 70 g of wine vinegar in a bowl. Let the onion slices soak for 15 to 20 minutes, stirring occasionally. At last, empty them.

Step Three

Slice everything extremely thin after trimming and peeling the cucumber and halving it lengthwise. Dice the tomatoes into tiny pieces.

Step Four

In a large bowl, crumble the soaked bread and squeeze lightly if it's very wet.

Step Number Five

After adding the onions that had been previously drained, combine the tomato cubes, cucumber slices, and finely chopped basil.

Step Six

Add the chopped anchovies (into six pieces).

Step 7

After letting the panzanella sit in the fridge for approximately an hour, season it with four tablespoons of oil, fifteen grams of vinegar, a dash of pepper, and a hefty amount of salt. Keep in mind that Tuscan bread lacks flavor, so if you're not using anchovies and capers, season liberally. To preserve the vegetable's texture if you prepare it the day before, don't season it.

Place the panzanella on the table and savor its flavors.

THE MEDITERRANEAN DIET COOKBOOK FOR BEGINNERS

Tabbouleh

Fresh and colourful, tabbouleh has long been a mainstay of Middle Eastern cooking, especially in Lebanon. It's a recipe that honors basic, healthful components, each of which contributes significantly to its distinct flavor and texture. Recognized for its vibrant, zesty flavor, tabbouleh is the ideal fusion of tomatoes, bulgur wheat, parsley, and a sharp lemon dressing.

Parsley is the key ingredient in tabbouleh—a lot of it. In contrast to most salads, where greens take back stage, parsley is the star of this one. It adds a fresh, slightly spicy flavor and makes up the majority of the salad when chopped finely. In addition to adding a brilliant freshness and a beautiful green hue, parsley gives Tabbouleh a wonderfully refreshing taste. Mint, which provides another layer of herbal taste and boosts the overall brightness of the salad, is frequently found with parsley.

Middle Eastern salads like tabbouleh are well-known for their bright, fresh flavors. The main ingredients are bulgur wheat, tomatoes, mint, onions, olive oil, lemon juice, and freshly chopped parsley. The salad's foundation ingredient, parsley, gives it a crisp, herbaceous flavor. The chewy texture and pleasing nuttiness of bulgur wheat are added. Mint leaves add a fragrant and refreshing tone, and diced tomatoes add juiciness and a hint of sweetness. Finely chopped onions add a bit of crunch and a subtle pungency. Rich olive oil and tart lemon juice make up the dressing, which unites the ingredients and improves the flavor profile overall. The end product is a tasty, light salad that is nourishing and refreshing.

The grain that is typically used to make tabbouleh is bulgur wheat. It's a kind of cracked, partially cooked, and dried whole wheat grain. Bulgur gives a mild, nutty flavor and a light, chewy texture after rehydrated. Bulgur is usually soaked rather than baked in tabbouleh, which keeps it fluffy and light while absorbing the flavors of the dressing made of lemon and olive oil. While bulgur is always present to add the necessary texture, some versions of the salad utilize less of it to keep the dish light and centered on the greens.

Another essential ingredient is tomatoes, which give the meal some juiciness and a touch of sweetness. Usually chopped finely to blend in with the bulgur and parsley's textures, they produce a pleasing blend of hues and flavors. To add extra crunch and refreshing, fresh cucumbers are frequently added to salads, adding more depth and diversity to each bite.

Tabbouleh dressing is very tasty and delightfully simple. It has a hint of salt and pepper and is created with extra virgin olive oil and fresh lemon juice. The olive oil adds a rich, velvety base that unifies all the elements in the salad, while the lemon juice adds a tart, biting flavor. The dressing's harmony of acidity and richness brings out the inherent flavors.

As an accompaniment to hummus, baba ganoush, and pita bread, tabbouleh is frequently relished as part of a mezze platter. However, it also pairs well as a side dish with grilled meats, falafel, or fish. For those seeking a filling and nutritious dinner, this is a terrific alternative because it's light, healthful, and nutrient-rich.

Recipe that works for me.

Of course, parsley! When I cook, I usually use Italian flat-leaf parsley, but sometimes I make an exception for tabbouleh. Here, the brighter color, tastier flavor, and lighter texture of curly parsley appeal to me.

Mint: It gives the salad a delightfully refreshing flavor.

For those who are unfamiliar, bulgur is essentially broken wheat that has been partially boiled before being dried. Traditionally, fine bulgur would be used to make tabbouleh, but because I can't seem to get it in my local grocery stores, I usually make the salad with coarse bulgur. Either will do; use whatever you can find.

Cucumber: For texture! Here, I prefer Persian and English cucumbers. I suggest peeling and seeding a standard cucumber if you're using one.

Tomatoes: They give the salad a luscious texture.

Garlic and scallions add an oniony flavor to the salad.

Cinnamon and coriander: For a rich, earthy flavor.

Fresh lemon juice and extra-virgin olive oil – They form a vibrant, tangy dressing for the salad.

And sea salt—to bring out every flavor!

The adaptability of tabbouleh is one of its charms. Although the classic form just uses a few essential ingredients, you can modify it to your preference. Some add extra veggies, such as onions or peppers, while others experiment with different grains, such as quinoa, to make a gluten-free version. Whatever your personal preferences, tabbouleh consistently offers a zesty, herbaceous, and refreshing taste that perfectly captures the essence of Middle Eastern and Mediterranean cuisine.

Salade Niçoise

The traditional French salad known as salade Niçoise comes from Nice, a sunny Mediterranean city. With its harmonious and fulfilling combination of fresh veggies, briny olives, and protein-rich tuna, it's the ideal depiction of the region's colourful cuisine. Salade Niçoise, which offers a lovely combination of healthful ingredients, is a meal in and of itself. It is renowned for its vibrant flavors, exquisite presentation, and variety of textures.

Salade Niçoise is essentially composed of just the finest, freshest ingredients. Traditionally, the salad has a bed of crunchy greens that give it a light and crunchy texture, such as butter lettuce or mixed field greens. But the dish's mix of veggies—especially the tomatoes, potatoes, and green beans—is what really makes it special. Usually, the green beans are blanched just long enough to keep their crunchy texture and vivid green color. To balance out the dish, tomatoes add a luscious sweetness, and new potatoes, when boiled until tender, bring a robust, creamy texture that contrasts wonderfully with the fresh vegetables.

Another essential component of Salade Niçoise is tuna, and the quality of this ingredient can significantly impact the outcome. Traditionally, tuna in a can with olive oil is utilized, which adds a deep, delicious dimension to the salad. For a more sophisticated approach, several contemporary versions now use grilled fresh tuna steaks. In any case, the tuna enhances the flavor of the veggies and other ingredients with a strong, meaty bite.

Without hard-boiled eggs, no Salade Niçoise could be considered complete. Typically, the eggs are cut in half or quarters, with the hard, mild contrast provided by the whites and the rich, creamy yolks imparting a hint of richness. Little, mildly bitter Niçoise olives give the tuna a saline, salty bite that accentuates the dish's Mediterranean flavor.

Anchovies are frequently added to salads, either tossed in or draped over the top, to add even more flavor. These elevate the salad with their flash of umami and punch of saltiness. Even though they are a contentious element, anchovies are traditional to the dish and offer a genuine taste of the area.

A basic vinaigrette consisting of olive oil, Dijon mustard, red wine vinegar, and a hint of garlic is the dressing for Salade Niçoise. It's tasty but not heavy, letting the natural freshness of the ingredients take center stage. The flavors are enhanced without being overpowered by the vinaigrette, which offers a tangy, somewhat sharp touch to bind everything together.

Salade Niçoise's adaptability is one of its many lovely qualities. There are endless variations depending on personal preferences or what's in season, even though the classic version is made with certain ingredients. Some recipes call for substituting grilled chicken or salmon for tuna, while others may call for adding extras like bell peppers, capers, or artichoke hearts. Fresh, vivid, and incredibly fulfilling is the essence of Salade Niçoise, whether you choose to follow the traditional recipe or add your own spin.

This salad works well as a summer meal's main course, a robust side, or even a light lunch. It looks as good as it tastes because of its brilliant presentation of carefully organized components and colourful veggies. A great blend of savory, fresh, and salty flavors, salade Niçoise delivers a sense of the Mediterranean in every bite. It's perfect for dining al fresco or anytime you want something light but filling.

The mixed greens plate Niçoise, pronounced "nee-Suarez," is essentially a French-style salad made of mixed greens, resembling our American Cobb plate but with potatoes, green beans, and fish instead of bacon, avocado, and chicken.

The mixed greens plate Niçoise originated in Nice, on the Mediterranean Sea, but like many other French-inspired foods that we like here, it has evolved to suit our tastes. Wikipedia states that the mixed greens served at Niçoise restaurants are always made with uncooked vegetables and accompanied with anchovies.

For 60 minutes, marinate fish steaks in a small amount of olive oil. Heat a large skillet over medium-high heat or place over a hot grill. Sear the steaks for two to three minutes on each side, or until well done.

How to make Salade Niçoise

1 To make the vinaigrette, combine the oil, mustard, herbs, shallots, lemon juice or vinegar, and other ingredients in a container. Cover and shake until thoroughly combined. To taste, add more salt and pepper.

2 Marinate onion slices in part of the vinaigrette: Spoon three tablespoons of the vinaigrette over the onion slices in a small bowl. (The onions will get thinner as a result of absorbing the

vinaigrette.)

3. Peel, chop, and toss with vinaigrette the potatoes: Put the potatoes in a large saucepan and cover with two quarts of water. Add one tablespoon of salt. Turn up the heat to high enough to boil. Reduce the heat to maintain a stew. Simmer the potatoes for ten to twelve minutes, or until they are tender to the fork. Channel.

Cut the potatoes into quarters or equal portions while they are still warm, depending on their size.

Place them in a bowl and drizzle about 1/4 cup of the vinaigrette over them.

4 Bring the green beans to a boil in salted water: While the potatoes are cooking, add two teaspoons of salt to a medium-sized pot and cover most of the way with water. Bring the mixture to a boil over high heat. Pour the boiling water over the green beans.

Simmer for 3 to 5 minutes, or until the beans are tender but still firm to the bite (around 5 minutes total, depending on how strong they are).

Deplete and either rinse under cold water to halt cooking, or shock with ice water for a significant amount of time.

5 Arrange on a bed of lettuce: Put some lettuce on a tray for serving. Cut fish into thick slices, about 1/2 inch. Hill fish in the center of the lettuce leaf. Arrange the onions and tomatoes so they rim the fish.

Organize the green beans and potatoes into hills near the lettuce's edge.

Arrange the hard-boiled eggs, olives, and anchovies (if using) in lettuce bed hills.

6 Pour the remaining vinaigrette over everything. Add an adventure sprinkle, if using.

Serve immediately. Should be served at room temperature or just slightly heated.

CHAPTER 5:

Soups & Stews

Gazpacho

The soup known as gazpacho is native to Andalusia in southern Spain. It is cold and pleasant. This chilled tomato-based soup delivers a rush of vibrant, fresh tastes with every spoonful, making it the ideal remedy for hot summer days. Light and pleasant, gazpacho is renowned for its simplicity and capacity to highlight the freshness of its fresh ingredients. Known variously as cold soup, salad, or smoothie, gazpacho is a popular summertime dish in Spain that is inexpensive, scrumptious, and quick to make.

Ripe tomatoes make up the foundation of a classic gazpacho; the riper, the better. Together with a few other traditional Mediterranean ingredients, these tomatoes offer a foundation of sweetness and tanginess. You can find onions, bell peppers, cucumbers, and garlic next to the tomatoes. Depending on your desire, the finely chopped or blended vegetables have a smooth or somewhat chunky texture. The garlic adds the perfect amount of sharpness, the bell peppers and onions offer depth of flavor, and the cucumbers bring a crisp freshness.

Gazpacho is distinguished from other cold soups by its distinct flavor and texture combination. A zesty vinaigrette consisting of extra virgin olive oil, vinegar, and a tiny pinch of salt elevates the fresh veggies. The vinegar (typically sherry vinegar) offers a strong, tangy brightness that accentuates the sweetness of the tomatoes and the freshness of the cucumbers, while the olive oil gives the soup a silky, rich mouthfeel. Gazpacho is incredibly addictive because of its flavor balance; every mouthful is a delicious combination of savory, tart, and slightly sweet flavors.

Bread is another necessary component of gazpacho. Stale bread is typically soaked in water and then mixed into the soup to add thickness and body. This bread base gives the dish a delicate, earthy flavor that unifies the entire dish in addition to helping to generate the ideal texture. You can easily omit the bread and still enjoy the refreshing flavor of gazpacho in a gluten-free form.

The adaptability of gazpacho is one of its lovely qualities. This is a dish that can readily be altered to suit your preferences or the ingredients you happen to have on hand. Some variants include a dash of jalapeño for a sense of spiciness, or you could even add fresh herbs like parsley or basil. Additionally, you can alter the texture; maintain-keep it chunky for more bite or blend it until completely smooth for a silky, drinkable soup.

Since gazpacho is usually served cold, it's a cool appetizer or light supper option for hot weather. It can be served in glasses to be consumed like a savory smoothie, or it can be poured into bowls and eaten with a spoon. You may garnish with chopped vegetables, croutons for crunch, or simply a splash of olive oil.

In addition to being extremely healthful, gazpacho is refreshing. Full of fresh veggies, it's a great way to get your vitamins, antioxidants, and fluids. It's a great option for a light summer lunch or as an appetizer to a larger dinner because it's satisfying but low in calories.

How to prepare gazpacho

For four servings, or just me, of a liter and a half of gazpacho

One kilogram of fully ripe tomatoes, preferably the Roma type.

One big cucumber.

1/2 a tiny sweet onion

1/2 a red pepper

1 ½ green pepper

1/2 a cup of extra virgin olive oil

1/4 cup vinegar made from white wine

1 couple of ice cubes

Add salt to taste.

Instruction

After immersing the tomatoes in boiling water for 15 seconds, allowing them to cool, and then peeling them by hand, the tomatoes should be readily removed. Cut.

Peel the onion and cucumbers. Cut.

Put some seeds in the peppers. Cut.

Add a little water to a blender and add all the chopped vegetables. Add the oil in a small stream while they combine. Incorporate the vinegar and approximately 0.5 tsp of salt.

For a few minutes, or until the mixture is smooth, blend the hell out of it at maximum speed. When the ice melts, add the ice cubes and mix at a medium speed. After tasting, adjust the salt.

Serve right away or store in the refrigerator for up to one day.

Optional: To provide a thicker texture, a common variant is to incorporate a slice of hard white bread into the mixture. Personally, I add a few shakes of Tabasco sauce or something similar, along with around half a teaspoon of ground cumin.

As an appetizer, an afternoon snack, or a smoothie after working out, gazpacho is ideal.

Have fun!

Soupe au Pistou

A classic Provençal vegetable soup from the south of France, soupe au Pistou is renowned for its cheery simplicity and bright, fresh aromas. This dish combines the essence of Mediterranean cooking—using fresh, healthful ingredients to produce something genuinely satisfying—with a celebration of the harvest of the season. This soup's standout feature is its fragrant pistou sauce, which is a cousin of Italian pesto and is swirled in at the very end to give the soup a burst of flavourful herbs.

Soupe au Pistou is essentially a vegetable soup, with slightly different additions based on what's available and in season. To make a thick and filling base, it usually consists of stewed green beans, zucchini, potatoes, carrots, and tomatoes. Because the veggies are cut into bite-sized bits, each mouthful delivers a variety of flavors and textures. The zucchini and green beans add a bright green color and a little crunch, and the potatoes give a creamy smoothness. The little acidity of the tomatoes counteracts the sweetness of the other veggies in the soup.

Apart from the veggies, Cannellini or White beans are frequently added to Soupe au Pistou to give it a creamy and protein-rich touch. Small pasta shapes, such macaroni or shells, may also be added to some recipes to give the soup a bit more body and structure. It's filling and comforting, the ideal ratio of lightness to heartiness thanks to the fresh veggies, beans, and pasta.

The pistou itself is what really distinguishes Soupe au Pistou. Pistou is a mixture of fresh basil, garlic, and olive oil, similar to Italian pesto but without the pine nuts. It is frequently topped with a hefty portion of grated Parmesan or Gruyère cheese. The end product is a silky, highly aromatic sauce that is poured into the steaming soup right before serving. The broth gains a delightfully aromatic, herb-forward taste from the heat of the soup, which also releases the oils from the garlic and basil. In addition to adding richness, the pistou changes the soup's flavor from basic and rustic to something quite exceptional.

Its adaptability is what makes Soupe au Pistou so beautiful. This is a dish that may be changed to fit your preferences or what's in season. While some cooks choose to skip the pasta for a lighter version, others can choose to add a few extra veggies, such as leeks or spinach. The pistou, with its strong, fresh flavor, unites all the other ingredients and is always the star of the show.

Although soupe au Pistou is best enjoyed warm, it tastes equally good at room temperature and is a terrific choice in any season. It's frequently eaten as a light but filling main meal, especially when it's accompanied by crusty French bread for dipping. Soupe du Pistou, a celebration of summer's bounty that offers a pleasantly fragrant and nutritious flavor of the south of France, is perfect for a leisurely lunch or as part of a bigger dinner.

This soup is a great way to demonstrate the simplicity, freshness, and flavor of Provençal cuisine while also providing nourishment to the body. Soupe au Pistou is a recipe that is ideal for informal get-togethers or family dinners, but it's also an invitation to enjoy the season, the table, and good company.

Fisherman's Stew

A stew that was traditionally made by fisherman, mainly using leftover fish parts. By the way, "fisherman" is too sexist in Canada, therefore a lot of people use "fishers," which is inclusive of both sexes. Some female fishermen, however, find the phrase offensive and would rather be called "fisherman" or "fisherwoman." The gender battles are like this.

A robust, rustic meal that embodies the spirit of coastal Mediterranean cuisine is Fisherman's Stew. It's a hearty, aromatic stew that combines a variety of seafood with a savory, thick broth to highlight the abundance of the sea. It's a hearty and filling dish that has the flavors of the sea, herbs, and spices in every bite.

Fisherman's stew's simplicity is its essence. This dish, which is traditionally prepared by fisherman using the day's fresh catch, is all about making the most of what is available and transforming it into something nourishing. Depending on the area or what's in season, the seafood may change, but it usually consists of a variety of white fish, mussels, clams, shrimp, and occasionally scallops or crab. Layers of taste and texture are added to the stew by the variety of seafood, from plump, salty shellfish to delicate fish flakes.

Rich, flavourful broth, commonly cooked with a mixture of tomatoes, garlic, onions, and white wine or fish stock, forms the foundation of the stew. The flavors of these ingredients combine to create a base that is fragrant and tasty as they are carefully cooked together. The garlic and onions offer depth and warmth, while the tomatoes balance the richness of the fish with a hint of sweetness and acidity. The seafood's marine taste is enhanced by the white wine or fish stock, resulting in a rich but delicate soup.

Fisherman's stew's taste profile also heavily relies on herbs and spices. Frequently used herbs that add a fragrant and herbal note to the dish include fresh parsley, thyme, or basil. There may be a hint of saffron in some variations, which gives the soup a little earthy flavor and a golden tint. To counterbalance the sweetness of the tomatoes and the brininess of the seafood, a sprinkle of paprika or red pepper flakes can add a light touch of spice.

The adaptability of Fisherman's Stew is one of its great qualities. You can modify it to suit your tastes or the ingredients you have on hand. Certain recipes call for extra heartiness, such as potatoes, fennel, or carrots; others are lighter and simpler, requiring only seafood and broth. You may also serve the stew with crusty bread on the side to mop up the savory liquid, or you can thicken it with a little piece of bread.

The smell of simmering seafood and herbs fills the kitchen during the process of making Fisherman's Stew, making it an immersive experience. Although it's a quick dish to make, the flavors seem to have been cooking for hours. To ensure that the seafood stays soft, it is added toward the conclusion of the cooking procedure.

Served with a squeeze of lemon for brightness and a sprinkle of fresh herbs, this stew is frequently consumed as a main meal. To soak up the flavourful soup, it goes well with a slice of warm, crusty bread and a glass of crisp white wine. A dish that offers a taste of the sea and a sense of coziness, Fisherman's stew is perfect for gatherings, whether they are served as part of a Mediterranean-inspired feast or on a cold evening.

In addition to celebrating the wealth of the ocean, Fisherman's Stew pays homage to the straightforward, sincere cooking of the fisherman who prepared it. It is ideal for both a laid-back family meal and a formal event. Bold yet well-balanced flavors make it a memorable dish that's both nourishing and delicious.

Ingredients

1 cup of San Marzano or other canned crushed tomatoes

1/4 tsp red pepper flakes, or according to taste

2 cups of water

1/8 ounce sea bass fillet

8 medium shrimp, skinned and deveined, but not cooked

8 ounces of tentacles and rings of calamari

12 debearded and cleaned mussels

12 cleaned clams in their shells

2 tsp butter

2 tsp olive oil

½ bulb of fennel, cored, sliced thinly, and with the fronds set aside

ROLL ALEX

4 garlic cloves, cut thinly

salt according to taste

1/2 a cup of white wine

1/2 a cup of newly cut parsley

Instruction

Step 1

In a measuring cup or bowl, combine tomatoes, red pepper flakes, and water. With an immersion blender, puree until smooth.

Step 2

Slice the sea bass into pieces that are about 1 1/2 inches in size, matching the other seafood. When ready to use, place sea bass, shrimp, calamari, mussels, and clams in separate dishes.

Step 3

In a deep pan set over medium-high heat, melt the butter and olive oil. Add the salt, garlic, and sliced fennel. Cook and stir for one minute, or until the garlic turns color. Add white wine and stir. Simmer for two to three minutes, or until reduced by roughly half. Add the tomato broth base, bring to a boil, and cook the fennel for two to three minutes, or until it is soft. Taste and adjust the seasonings.

Step 4

- Stir in parsley, sea bass, shrimp, and calamari. Add clams and mussels. Cover, increase heat to high, and cook until clam and mussel shells open and sea bass, shrimp, and calamari are opaque, about 5 minutes.

Step 5
Move to serving bowls that are heated. Serve with the reserved fennel fronds as a garnish.

Avgolemono

What is meant by the term "avgolemono"?
Avgo Gr. αυγό = egg

λέμονο from λεμόνι = lemon is Lemono Gr.

When cooking, eggs and lemons are combined.

The most well-known soup, and the soup queen in my book, is

avgolemoni, which is made with rice and chicken foam.

has a delicious flavor and is really nutritious.

However, the mixture can also be utilized in other recipes, like staff cabbage, vine leaves, and mutton.

A typical Greek soup, avagolemono is distinguished by its vibrant, acidic flavor and creamy texture even though it is created with a few basic ingredients. "Egg-lemon" is how the Greek word "avgolemono" actually means, and it sums up this dish's flavor well. This hearty and adaptable soup is frequently served as an appetizer or even as a light dinner on its own.

Avgolemono is essentially a broth-based soup that is thickened with eggs and seasoned with freshly squeezed lemon juice, giving it a rich but not overly thick texture. The soup has a distinct, cool taste from the eggs and lemon, which perfectly counterbalances the warmth of the broth. The outcome is reassuring and energizing, making it ideal for any time of year.

Traditionally, a base of chicken broth is used to make avgolemono, giving the dish a thick, savory base. To give the soup more body and substance, some variations incorporate rice or orzo, a tiny noodle. In order to absorb the flavor of the stock and contribute to the soup's distinctive heartiness, the rice or pasta is cooked right in the broth until it becomes soft.

The egg-lemon mixture added near the end of cooking is what gives avgolemono its enchantment. This is made by whisking eggs and lemon juice together until the mixture is creamy and foamy. Then, in a step known as tempering, a small amount of the warm broth is gradually mixed into the egg mixture to keep the eggs from scrambling when added to the hot soup. This is the secret to getting the soup's opulent, creamy texture without using any dairy or cream.

The egg-lemon mixture thickens and adds that distinctive silkiness to the soup once it is completely combined with the broth. The dish is elevated by the zesty, lemony freshness of the freshly squeezed lemon juice, which cuts through the richness of the eggs. Its flavors—rich, creamy, tangy, and savory—are well balanced.

Additionally, there are numerous ways to modify Avgolemono. Although chicken broth is typically used to make the traditional version, veggie or fish broth can also be used. Certain dishes incorporate pieces of shredded chicken, adding to the meal's fillingness. The fact that avgolemono is served as a sauce instead of a soup in some parts of Greece demonstrates the dish's versatility.

The simplicity and the way that just a few staple ingredients—eggs, lemon, broth, and rice—can combine to create something so elegant yet comfortable characterize avgolemono. This recipe is satisfying and light at the same time, making it ideal for a cool soup on a warm evening or for warming up on a chilly day.

A classic comfort food, avgolemono is topped with fresh herbs like dill or parsley and is typically served with crusty bread on the side. It is the epitome of Greek home cuisine. Avgolemono's creamy, tangy richness will wow guests whether you serve it as a sophisticated appetizer for a Mediterranean-inspired dinner or as a comforting supper when you're feeling under the weather.

Italian Bean and Bacon Stew

Rich, savory tastes abound in this substantial, rustic dish called Italian Bean and Bacon Stew, which is made with basic ingredients. Famous for its capacity to elevate simple beans and smokey bacon to a rich and savory dish that's ideal for a cosy evening or chilly weather, this stew is a mainstay of Italian cooking.

Essentially, white beans—typically cannellini or borlotti beans—are used to make this stew because of their mild flavor and creamy texture. The focal point of the meal is these beans, which give the stew its thick, velvety consistency while they absorb the flavourful broth and other components. The base of this hearty stew is beans, whether you use canned beans for ease of use or dried beans that have been soaked overnight.

This dish's distinct depth and smokiness come from the bacon addition. The bacon releases fat while it cooks, giving the stew a flavourful richness that melds well with the beans. The bacon contrasts the creamy texture of the beans with its crispy edges and meaty bite, adding both texture and flavor. For an even more authentic Italian touch, pancetta—Italian cured pork belly—may be used in place of bacon in certain varieties.

Traditional Italian aromatics such as onion, garlic, celery, and carrots are sautéed in the bacon fat to form the rich base and contribute to the overall flavor of the stew. The subtle sweetness and depth that these vegetables bring balances the richness of the beans and bacon. For a subtle heat boost, a dash of black pepper or crushed red pepper flakes is frequently added, which enhances the dish's appeal.

The broth is a crucial component of the Italian Bean and Bacon Stew. The broth, which is typically produced from chicken or vegetable stock, unifies everything and brings out the tastes of the aromatics, bacon, and beans. To give the stew a lovely ruby hue and a hint of tanginess, some recipes ask for adding chopped or crushed tomatoes. In addition, the tomatoes' slight acidity counteracts the bacon's richness.

The flavors blend together in the stew as it simmers, producing a hearty, filling dish that can be eaten on its own or with a slice of crusty bread to mop up the tasty liquid. A crucial component of the meal is the bread, which provides a crisp texture to balance the soft beans and smokey bacon.

The adaptability of Italian Bean and Bacon Stew is one of its best features. For more nutrients and color, you can add other veggies like kale, spinach, or zucchini. You may even replace the bacon with ham or sausage to vary the flavor while keeping the spirit of something hearty and warm.

Because its flavors intensify and meld over the course of a day or two in the refrigerator, this stew makes a fantastic make-ahead meal. It's ideal for bulk cooking and freezing for later use. It's also great for meal planning. Bring the warmth and tastes of Italy to your table with this crowd-pleasing recipe for Italian Bean and Bacon Stew, perfect for a casual dinner party with friends or family.

This dish, which celebrates the beauty of Italian cooking in every spoonful, is both rustic and elegant. Serve it with a simple green salad and a glass of red wine.

Ingredients.

Four thickly sliced bacon strips

One teaspoon of unsalted butter

One onion, chopped and peeled

Two celery stalks, chopped

Two large carrots, cut into cubes and peel

One tablespoon of flour (all purpose)

Four cups of chicken stock

4 cups cooked white beans

chopped chives (optional) as a garnish

grated Parmesan cheese (optional) as a garnish

To taste, add salt and black pepper.

Instruction,

*In a large soup pot over medium heat, cook the bacon until crispy. To remove all but a tablespoon of the bacon fat, place the bacon on a dish covered with paper towels.

* Add the chopped carrots, celery, and onion, and sauté for a few minutes, or until the vegetables start to soften. After pushing the veggies to the pot's edges, stir in the flour and melt in the tablespoon of butter.

*After adding the beans, whisk in the chicken stock. After bringing to a boil, cover, turn down the heat, and simmer for 30 minutes. Puree roughly half of the soup with a stick blender (you can also use a conventional blender), leaving it as chunky as you like.

 A potato masher can be used for this, but the consistency won't be as smooth. To taste, add salt and pepper for seasoning.

Garnish with grated Parmesan cheese, bacon crumbles, and chives and serve hot.

CHAPTER 6:

Sides & Dips

Tzatziki Dip

The Tzatziki Dip is one of the popular Mediterranean dishes with a creamy texture and tangy taste that is really beautiful and easy to enjoy. It can be seen across many Greek dishes and this is the one which adds moisture and gives brightness to many dishes whether it is grilled meat or fresh veggies.

Tzatziki is a dip consisting of salted strained yogurt with cucumber. it is made of strained yogurt, shredded cucumber, oil, soybean, garlic, lemon, salt, and herbs. The traditional tzatziki in Greece has sheep's or goat yogurt while I use normal full fat greek yogurt for my tzatziki recipe. It is more readily available in the market and has that nice thick creamy consistency which is required in tzatziki sauce. Aside from the other normal ingredients, fresh dill and mint leaves are added up to give off a nice summer taste.

Greek yogurt is the main ingredient in tzatziki, giving the dip its thick, creamy basis. Greek yogurt gives tzatziki an opulent texture that makes it so delicious since it is thicker and more concentrated than plain yogurt. The yogurt's tanginess complements the other ingredients well and contributes to the dip's distinctive flavor profile.

How to Make Tzatziki Sauce

The first time I tasted tzatziki was in Greek restaurants, but I quickly found out that this sauce is very simple to prepare. Zuluyu, together with pesto, is one of the summertime sauces I always make at least once. And here is how you do it:

The first step would be to take the cucumber and grate it. I use big holes on a box grater so as to give my final sauce some texture with plenty of green flecks in it.

Then comes the next step which is to remove the water from the grated cucumber. This step is very important if you want to come up with a thick tzatziki. If you don't do this step, the water from the cucumber will separate your sauce. Squeeze the cucumber into the sink or over the sink, or step in between two kitchen towels or paper towels and lightly press. .

Last but not least, everyone stir Uncle Bob's food together with a spoon, and it's already delicious. Mix the squeezed cucumber with yogurt, lemon juice, garlic, olive oil, salt, herbs, and refrigerate until you need it.

That's exactly right!

Tzatziki Preparation

Application of Tzatziki

There are a multitude of options for making use of the spread after it has been prepared. The simplest of all is to simply dip fresh cut vegetables or pita bread crackers or chips. Try out this recipe, or add this to the next crudites platter you serve for your friends. They will adore it!

Another good alternative is to make use of it in sandwiches for instance, pita wraps as well as presenting it with a Mediterranean salad for example a tabouleh or a couscous salad. Now, as a final thing, serve

Tzatziki has a wide range of uses. The most popular way to eat it is as a dip for veggies, pita bread, or grilled chicken or lamb. It goes well with Mediterranean feasts because of its cool, creamy texture, which acts as the appropriate counterpoint to rich, savory meals. Tzatziki is a refreshing and flavourful addition that can enhance any meal, whether it is served as a topping for a gyro sandwich or combined with a platter of meze.

The ease of making tzatziki at home is one of its many wonderful qualities. Thanks to the base of protein-rich yogurt and hydrating cucumber, you can make a dip that is not only tasty but also healthful with just a few simple ingredients and a short mix. It's a luxurious-feeling dip.

Tzatziki Dip is a staple, whether you're eating it as a snack with raw vegetables or serving it as part of a Mediterranean-inspired meal. It's the kind of meal that everyone enjoys because of its zesty, refreshing flavor and capacity to enhance whatever it's served with.

Romesco Sauce

Romesco is a thick, rich sauce made from roasted red peppers and charred tomatoes that is puréed and thickened with bread and toasted almonds. The flavors are further enhanced with the addition of raw garlic, vinegar, chile powder or red pepper flakes (tune the heat to your preference). The end product is a strong, smoky sauce that is typically served with fish and mild-mannered vegetables. (A grilled vegetable feast, according to some Spaniards, is just an excuse to eat romesco.) However, the sauce tastes as delicious when applied to bread that has been drizzled with olive oil and then rubbed with extra garlic. To enhance the taste melding process, if possible, let the sauce at room temperature for an hour before serving.

Roasted red peppers and tomatoes are the main ingredients of romesco, giving the sauce its distinctive color and flavor—sweet and smokey. The backbone of the sauce is these roasted veggies, which add a rich, deep flavor that is counterbalanced with a hint of natural sweetness. Romesco is a well balanced sauce because the tomatoes give acidity and the peppers add a hint of fire.

The toasted almonds or hazelnuts are one of the main components that distinguish romesco from other sauces. These ground nuts give the sauce a unique texture and nutty depth of flavor when combined with the sauce. Romesco's robustness and distinctive richness come from the almonds that give it its heartiness and make it more than just a sauce for your food.

This is a traditional Spanish sauce, created with a variety of nuts (almonds and hazelnuts) and red peppers. Tomatoes, garlic, onions, red wine vinegar, and a few other ingredients and thickeners are also frequently used.

One of the best things about Romesco sauce is how versatile it is. Although it is typically eaten with grilled fish, especially in Catalonia where it goes very well with seafood, it has many other applications. Try it as a spread for sandwiches, a topping for grilled meats like chicken or lamb, or even as a dip for roasted potatoes. Its roasted veggies, such as broccoli, cauliflower, or asparagus, go incredibly well with its smoky, nutty flavor, which makes it a great addition to vegetarian dishes.

Ingredients

2 or 3 cored tomatoes (5 1/5 ounces or 150 grams each) (see note)

1 medium head of garlic, cut in half and without skin

Ancho chili peppers (about 3) or ñora peppers (about 4) dry, 1 ounce (30g); (see note)

1/2 ounce (40g) slice of stale or toasted bread, with the crusts cut off and the bread split into small pieces.

1 tablespoon (15ml) of sherry or red wine vinegar, or more if preferred

1/2 cup (2 3/4 ounces; 80g) peeled and toasted almonds or hazelnuts; (see remark)

2 tablespoons (30 milliliters) of extra virgin olive oil, or more, to taste

salt that is kosher

Instruction

1. Turn the oven on to 350°F, or 180°C. Arrange half of the garlic head and the tomatoes on an aluminum foil-lined baking sheet. Roast in the oven for approximately an hour, or until the garlic is tender and the tomatoes are wrinkled and lightly browned in places. Allow to cool.

2. In the meantime, put the dried peppers in a medium heat-resistant bowl and pour boiling water over them. To assist with submerging the peppers, place a weight or moist paper towel on top. Allow to stand for 30 to 1 hour, or until peppers are completely soft. Thick-skinned ñora peppers can be extremely obstinate, so you might need to rip a tiny hole in them so that water can get inside.

3. After draining, remove the peppers' seeds and stems. Carefully remove the flesh from the skins with a paring knife. Throw away the skins. Remove the peels from roasted garlic and tomatoes.

4. Using a Mortar and Pestle to Make Sauce: Place one or two peeled raw garlic cloves and three roasted garlic cloves in a mortar. (You are welcome to alter the amount of roasted or raw garlic in this recipe to suit your personal tastes.) Use a pestle to grind garlic into a paste.

5. Pour in the bread and wet it with vinegar. Reduce to a paste by smashing. Once added, finely break the nuts. When you're done, the mixture should resemble a rough paste.

6. Add the scraped pepper meat and roast the tomatoes, peeling them first. Add olive oil and stir until well incorporated. Add some salt for seasoning. If you would like a thinner, richer sauce, add extra oil, 1 tablespoon (15ml) at a time. To taste, add additional

vinegar as well.

7. Using an Immersion Blender or Countertop Blender to Make Sauce: Put 3 roasted garlic cloves and 2 raw garlic cloves that have been peeled into the blender jar, or blending container if you're using an immersion blender. (You can adjust the amount of roasted and raw garlic to suit your tastes.) Include nuts. Process until finely blended, stopping to scrape down the sides as needed.

8. Add the scraped pepper meat and peeled roasted tomatoes and blend. Blend in the vinegar, bread, and olive oil until smooth. (You can choose how smooth it is; some texture is acceptable.) Add salt for seasoning, and taste and adjust with additional oil and vinegar.

9. How to Use a Food Processor to Make Sauce: In the bowl of a food processor, blend 3 cloves roasted garlic and 2 cloves peeled raw garlic (use more or less roasted and raw garlic, as desired, according to your personal tastes), along with bread and almonds. Process until finely chopped, scraping down sides as needed.

10. Process the pepper meat and peeled roasted tomatoes together until a thick, coarse mixture is formed. Add the vinegar and olive oil, process, and season with salt. As needed, increase the vinegar and olive oil to change the texture and flavor.

To put it briefly, you just must have Romesco Sauce in your kitchen. It is a favorite of anyone wishing to add a hint of Mediterranean flair to their meals because of its rich and robust flavors and versatility in cooking.

Couscous Salad

A tasty and light dish that works well for practically any occasion, couscous salad strikes a balance between healthful grains and fresh toppings. This salad is full of flavors, colors, and textures that make it a pleasant and very adaptable dish that can be eaten as a side dish or on its own.

Couscous, a tiny, steamed semolina noodle that cooks quickly and absorbs flavors beautifully, is the star of this dish. Couscous is an ideal salad foundation since it cooks to a light and fluffy texture. Because of its mild flavor, it can absorb the flavors of the other components and provide a delicate, neutral background that accentuates stronger flavors.

The vivid and delicious meal that is created when fresh vegetables, herbs, and occasionally proteins are combined with couscous makes it truly unique. Vegetables including bell peppers, cucumbers, cherry tomatoes, and red onions are frequently used in couscous salads. With the crunch, sweetness, and little bite that these fresh veggies provide to the dish, each bite combines a variety of flavors and textures.

The versatility of couscous salad is one of its many wonderful qualities. It's simple to alter the recipe to your preferences. For instance, adding goat cheese or feta crumbles adds a creamy, tangy flavor that goes well with the veggies. To add a touch of sweetness, you might also add dried fruits like raisins or apricots. To make it a heartier dinner, you could even add grilled chicken or chickpeas.

Because the flavors of couscous salad tend to merge and get better with time, it's a great dish to make ahead of time. It works well as a light lunch, meal prep, picnics, and barbecues. This is the kind of meal that goes well on any table whether it is served cold or at room temperature.

Ingredients

Couscous: To make the salad, I use instant Moroccan couscous. It is typically seen in grocery stores and is quite little. Because it has been precooked through steaming, dried, and packaged, stovetop preparation is quick.

Vegetables: I use a variety of vibrant, differently-textured vegetables to add excitement to the salad. Red bell peppers, red onions, diced English cucumbers, and Roma tomatoes go well together.

Beans: To add more protein and fiber, try adding creamy canned garbanzo beans, sometimes referred to as chickpeas.

Kalamata olives: They impart a saline flavor. To make slicing easier, get the products that have been pitted.

Cheese: Feta cheese, which is salty and tangy, is crumbled on top as a garnish.

Herbs: Chopped parsley, mint, and basil are examples of fresh herbs that offer a powerful flavor and scent. To provide a more intense note, I add dried oregano.

Dressing: To make the lemon dressing, just combine olive oil, red wine vinegar, zest and juice of lemons, salt, and pepper.

Recipe for Couscous Salad

Step 1: Cook the couscous.

I prepare the instant couscous on the stovetop using my simple 5-minute method. In a saucepan, bring the water, salt, and olive oil to a boil. Add the couscous, cover, reduce the heat, and let the grains absorb the liquid. Using a fork, fluff it up to separate it. To cook the couscous rapidly, transfer it to a bowl and place it in the refrigerator. The fresh salad items will lose their structure if you mix heated couscous with them.

Step 2; Assemble the Salad

It's time to put the salad ingredients together once the couscous has cooled. The couscous, tomatoes, cucumbers, bell peppers, garbanzo beans, red onions, olives, cheese, parsley, mint, basil, and oregano should all be combined in a big bowl.

Step 3: Make the Lemon Dressing

Mix the citrus, vinegar, salt, and pepper in a small bowl. The salad gets its sharpness from the combination of red wine vinegar, fresh lemon zest, and juice. To quickly emulsify a dressing, whisk in the extra virgin olive oil.

Step 4: Garnish and Serve

Over the salad, drizzle with the dressing and toss lightly to mix. I like to add fresh herbs and extra feta as garnish. Just enough is made in the lemon dressing recipe to coat the ingredients.

In conclusion, couscous salad is a flavourful, light, and incredibly adaptable dish. Featuring a bed of light couscous, colourful veggies, fresh herbs, and a sharp lemon dressing, this dish is a straightforward yet sophisticated way to add Mediterranean flavors to your meal. A staple dish that's simple to customize to your tastes, couscous salad is ideal for warm weather or as an accompaniment to grilled meats.

Roast Brussels Sprouts

A straightforward but incredibly effective way to prepare this sometimes overlooked vegetable is to roast Brussels sprouts. Brussels sprouts magically convert from a thick, rather bitter vegetable to a crispy, caramelized, flavor-filled treat when roasted.

At their core, Brussels sprouts have a mild, nutty flavor, and roasting them brings out their natural sweetness. This way of cooking allows the exterior leaves to crisp up wonderfully, while the inside remains delicate, producing a perfect contrast in texture with every bite.

The secret to delicious roast Brussels sprouts is to prepare ahead of time. First, clip off any ends and remove any leaves that appear damaged on the outside. Slice larger sprouts in half, leaving smaller ones whole, for consistent cooking. Toss them in olive oil to make sure they crisp up, then add salt and pepper to taste. Not only does the olive oil help them brown in the oven, but it also gives them a richer flavor.

In an oven that has been preheated to around 400°F (200°C), roast the Brussels sprouts. It's the intense heat that gives them their lovely caramelization. The natural sugars in the sprouts start to caramelize as they roast, counteracting the slightly bitter flavors. When they get golden brown, with crispy edges and a soft center, which normally happens in 20 to 30 minutes, you will know they are done.

When the sprouts are almost done roasting, you can add some garlic cloves or Parmesan cheese for more taste. Just before serving, squeeze in some lemon juice to cut through the richness of the roasted sprouts and add a fresh, acidic contrast. If you're feeling very daring, you can also roast the sprouts and then sprinkle them with honey or balsamic sauce to provide a subtle sweetness that accentuates the flavor of the caramelized sprouts.

Not only are roast Brussels sprouts wonderful, but they're also very adaptable. They are a great side dish for any meal; they go well with seafood, roasted meats, and even vegetarian spreads. You can even use them in salads or toss them with crispy bacon, toasted almonds, or dried cranberries to make a more complicated dish.

In conclusion, roast Brussels sprouts are a tasty, healthful side dish that combines a pleasing variety of textures and flavors and is simple to make. They'll look great on your dinner table whether you dress them up with extra flavors or leave them simple with olive oil, salt, and pepper.

Ingredients

Fresh Brussels sprouts: Look for bright green, rather firm sprouts; avoid those with a lot of wilted leaves on the outside. See my Roasted Frozen Brussels Sprouts recipe if you want to make this recipe using frozen veggies.

Extra virgin olive oil coats each sprout and aids in their nice oven crisping. If you must make roasted Brussels sprouts without oil, I suggest substituting 2 teaspoons of soy sauce and skipping the additional salt.

Instruction

Combine 1/8 cup of toasted sesame oil, 1/4 cup honey, and 1/8 cup of balsamic reduction (thicken with a little bit of quality balsamic vinegar, cooking it down to an eighth of a cup).

Gently reheat everything together and add in the roasted Brussels sprouts. If you did not season the sprouts before roasting, you could want to add a little pinch of fine sea salt.

Icelandic course flake, Maldon sea salt, or the ever popular Carmague Fleur de Sel are Good possibilities, while the Maldon sea salt is a staple that most well stocked kitchens should keep on hand.

As always, best

CHAPTER 7:

Snacks

Quinoa Crispbread

Quinoa Crispbread is a tasty and wholesome snack option that lets you reap the health benefits of quinoa without sacrificing taste. It's an excellent substitute for ordinary crackers in terms of health, and it also works well as a base for a variety of toppings, both savory and sweet. Quinoa crispbread is unique because of its flavor, texture, and health advantages.

Because quinoa is a superfood that is packed in fiber, protein, and vital amino acids, this crispbread is not only delicious but also incredibly nourishing. Because it is gluten-free, it is perfect for people who are trying to reduce their intake of processed grains or who have a sensitivity to gluten.

The first step in making quinoa crispbread is to cook the quinoa and then add binding ingredients. Some recipes contain a blend of seeds like chia, flax, or sesame, which not only offer more texture but also improve the fiber and omega-3 content. You can also add a touch of olive oil to give the crispbread a rich, delicious taste.

After the mixture is ready, it is evenly distributed thinly onto a baking sheet so that the crispbread bakes evenly. Lowering the temperature and baking for longer is the secret to getting that ideal crispy texture. This prevents burning and enables the quinoa and seeds to dry completely, resulting in a crisp, cracker-like texture.

Quinoa crispbread is incredibly versatile, which is its charm. Its mildly nutty flavor goes well with a broad range of toppings. For a savory snack, you can have it with hummus, avocado, or cheese. Try it with fresh berries or nut butter and a honey drizzle for a sweeter touch. It also adds a delicious crunch to soups and salads, making it a great companion.

Due to its high protein and fiber content, quinoa crispbread is a fantastic alternative for a light lunch or as a midday snack. It also helps you feel full and satisfied. It's also a handy, portable snack that you can take with you wherever you go, ideal for a rapid, healthful energy boost.

Quinoa crispbread is essentially a healthy, crunchy snack that is simple to incorporate into a diet that is balanced. Whether you're eating it as part of a light breakfast, packing it for a weekday snack, or serving it alongside a bowl of soup, it's a great way to enjoy the health benefits of quinoa in a convenient, crispy form.

THE MEDITERRANEAN DIET COOKBOOK FOR BEGINNERS

Italian Caprese Bites

Italian Caprese Bites are a straightforward yet sophisticated appetizer that perfectly encapsulates Mediterranean flavors in a single, delicious mouthful. These bite-sized variations of the classic Caprese salad are ideal for gatherings, as light snacks, or as a component of an antipasti platter. In addition to being aesthetically pleasing and simple to put together, they combine colourful, fresh ingredients in a delicious and nutritious way.

Caprese skewers are a beautiful example of Italian culinary expertise; they are simple yet high-quality. This traditional recipe honors the well-known Caprese salad, a mainstay of Italian cooking. Caprese skewers transform classic ingredients like fresh tomatoes, creamy mozzarella, and aromatic basil into bite-sized gourmet marvels by combining their brilliant colors and aromas. Let's delve into the fascinating background and enjoy the recipe that has made caprese skewers a global favorite among foodies.

The simplicity of caprese bites is what makes them so beautiful. Just a few high-quality ingredients are required: extra virgin olive oil, fresh mozzarella, juicy cherry tomatoes, and basil leaves. These components, which have a refreshing and gratifying mix of flavor and texture, are classics in Italian cooking.

The Campania region in southern Italy is where Caprese salad first appeared, and this is where Caprese skewers got their start. The name of the salad is a reference to the gorgeous island of Capri, which is well-known for its Mediterranean appeal. The iconic colors of the salad—red, white, and green—mirror the Italian flag and stand for the pride and gastronomic legacy of the country. The Caprese salad gave rise to many variations over time, such as these delicious skewers.

The first step in assembling the bites is to thread a mozzarella ball, cherry tomato, and basil leaf onto toothpicks or tiny skewers. In addition to being visually appealing, this combination of the creamy mozzarella, juicy tomatoes, and fragrant fresh basil creates a delightful contrast of sensations.

The tastes are enhanced without being overpowered by a small drizzle of olive oil and a splash of balsamic glaze, which give the bites richness and depth. For extra spice, you may also add a little pinch of sea salt and freshly ground black pepper.

Ingredients and Variations: The simplicity of these skewers, each selected for its outstanding quality, is what makes them so beautiful. A balsamic glaze, a sprinkling of sea salt, and a spray of extra virgin olive oil are common ways to elevate the classic combination of tomatoes, mozzarella, and basil. Though the traditional pairing never goes out of style, contemporary interpretations could add prosciutto, olives, or a hint of pesto. Preserving a delicate balance that lets the essential ingredients take center stage is crucial.

Ingredients

Half a cherry tomato

new mozzarella sticks

fresh leaves of basil

Extra virgin olive oil

Balsamic reduction

To taste, add black pepper and sea salt.

wooden skewers

Instructions

1. Put a mozzarella ball, a cherry tomato, and a folded basil leaf on each skewer.
2. Continue doing this until you have the appropriate number of Caprese bits on the skewers.
3. Place the skewers on a board or serving plate.
4. Over the skewers, drizzle some extra virgin olive oil and balsamic glaze.
5. To taste, add a pinch of sea salt and black pepper.
6. Savor the taste harmonies by serving right away.

Simply put, Italian Caprese Bites highlight the best aspects of

Mediterranean cuisine with their ideal balance of simple, fresh ingredients. These bite-sized treats will wow guests with their elegance and flavor, whether you're holding a party or you just want a delicious and healthful snack.

Spiced Nuts

Spiced Nuts are a tasty and filling snack that give regular nuts a dash of warmth and excitement. Spiced nuts are an excellent choice for a party snack, a nutritious snack, or an appetizer to go with drinks. They have the perfect balance of spicy, savory, crunchy, and sweet flavors to keep things interesting.

Spiced nuts are beautiful because of how versatile they are. Any kind of nut will work well to start, whether it's almonds, cashews, pecans, walnuts, or a combination of your faves. Your choice of spices and seasonings will bring out the unique flavor and texture of each type of nut.

When making spiced nuts, you usually combine spices with oil (such as coconut or olive oil) and coat the nuts before roasting them in the oven. Popular seasonings for seasoned nuts include chili powder, paprika, cinnamon, cayenne, and cumin. A dash of sea salt will bring out all the flavors, and you can also add a little brown sugar or maple syrup for a hint of sweetness to counterbalance the spicy.

The ability to tailor spiced nuts to your preferences is one of their main features. Add more cayenne or chili flakes if you like your food hotter. To add a hint of smoke, smoked paprika is a great choice. If you want something sweeter and more comforting, use cinnamon and your nuts can become a festive snack with a dash of nutmeg.

Roasting the nuts releases their wonderful crunch and makes the spices stick to their surface, creating an irresistible coating that makes every bite full of flavor. The deep roast aroma of the nuts and the spices come to life, making this easy snack something special.

Roasted nuts are also very convenient; they can be prepared ahead of time, kept in an airtight container, and eaten all week long. They work well for on-the-go snacking, salad dressings, and cheese and charcuterie platters.

Ingredients

- 1 cup of uncooked pecans
- 1 cup of uncooked walnuts
- 1 1/2 tablespoons of melted olive or coconut oil
- 2 tablespoons of coconut sugar (plus more for garnish)
- 1 teaspoon powdered cinnamon
- 1 moderate pinch of cayenne
- 1 dash of ground nutmeg
- 1/4 teaspoon sea salt
- 2 tsp split maple syrup

Instructions

1. Preheat the oven to 350 degrees Fahrenheit (176 degrees Celsius). Transfer the pecans and walnuts to a bare (or parchment-lined) baking sheet (or multiple baking sheets if the quantity of the batch is larger).
2. Drizzle with oil, coconut sugar, cinnamon, cayenne, nutmeg, salt, and half of the maple syrup (1 Tbsp as directed in the original recipe; adjust if batch size).
3. Toss to coat. Bake for a total of 12 to 15 minutes, or until golden brown and fragrant, tossing or stirring once halfway through to ensure even cooking. Remove from oven and drizzle with the remaining maple syrup (1 Tbsp as directed in the original recipe; adjust if batch size). Optionally, you can add a little more salt, cinnamon, and coconut sugar to coat.
4. Mix well to coat, then serve warm or allow to dry out completely on the pan (they will crisp up) before storing in an airtight container for up to two weeks at

room temperature (or one month in the freezer).

5. These are a great little snack or topping for dishes like roasted sweet potatoes, smoothies, salads, and oats. They also create a beautiful present! Transfer into tiny jars, fasten with string or ribbon, and offer the goodness of plants as a gift.

To sum up, spiced nuts are the ideal snack since they mix flavor, crunch, and nutrients. They are simple to prepare, adaptable, and a hit at any gathering, regardless of your preference for them being sweet, spicy, or somewhere in between. Store a jar of them in your cupboard for an easy, healthful, and entertaining snack!

Date and Walnut Energy Bars

The year 2024 is almost here, and if you're like most people, you've probably thought about eating healthily and cleanly. My next dish, a "Dates and Nuts Bar," is perfect for any resolution you may have for the new year. This nutritious energy bar is sugar-free, vegan, and gluten-free. The bars taste amazing and have a lovely nutty texture. This delicious dessert will satisfy all of your sweet tooth needs!

Energy bars with dates and walnuts are a tasty and wholesome way to start the day. When you need a fast energy boost or something healthy to keep you going between meals, these handmade bars mix the natural sweetness of dates with the rich, earthy crunch of walnuts.

Date and Walnut Energy Bars are unique because of their potent ingredients and straightforward composition. Rich in naturally occurring sugars like fructose and glucose, dates are nature's candy because they give you energy right away without the crash that comes with refined sugars. Additionally, they are high in fiber, potassium, and magnesium, which promote healthy digestion and constant energy levels.

Conversely, walnuts are a great source of omega-3 fatty acids, which lower inflammation and support brain function. They are also a great source of healthy fats and protein, which helps you feel satiated for extended periods of time.

These bars are quite easy to prepare. Usually, the base that binds the bars together is made by first blending pitted dates into a smooth, sticky paste. After that, the chopped walnuts are added to the date paste to give it taste and texture. To improve the bars' taste and nutritional value, you can also add extras like oats, chia seeds, cocoa powder, or a small teaspoon of sea salt.

After combining all the ingredients, press the dough into a baking dish or form it into bars, then refrigerate to set. These bars are a quick and hassle-free solution because they don't require baking. Once they harden, you can slice them into bite-sized pieces and keep them in an airtight receptacle for quick snacking anytime you need it.

These bars have so many uses. They work well as pre- or post-workout snacks, but they can serve as a guilt-free, healthy dessert or midday energy boost. Compared to other energy bars found in stores, they are far healthier because they don't require any additional sugars because the dates naturally sweeten them.

Ingredients

1 half-cup of pitted dates, chopped into little pieces

2 tablespoons of cocoa powder

1/4 cup powdered coconut

1/3 cup flaxseed meal

1/3 teaspoon sea salt

½ cup finely chopped roasted walnuts; ½ cup finely chopped roasted almonds; ½ cup finely chopped roasted cashews; 2 tsp sesame seeds

Two teaspoons of pumpkin seeds

THE MEDITERRANEAN DIET COOKBOOK FOR BEGINNERS

Instructions

1. Microwave the chopped dates for 30 seconds to soften them and make them workable.
2. In the food processor, pulse the dates until they form a paste; this should take approximately 15 seconds. In the food processor, add the flex seed meal, cocoa powder, and salt. Process until all the ingredients are combined. This ought to take fifteen seconds or so.
3. Add the cashew, walnut, and almond nuts that have

been toasted and diced. Blended for about 20 seconds, or until all the ingredients were combined, but the nuts should still be chunky.

4.Take the mixture out of the food processor, form it into two balls, roll it into a 1/4-inch thick roll, and then top the rolled bar with sesame and pumpkin seeds.

Carrot Cake Energy Balls

Carrot Cake Energy Balls are a nutrient-dense, bite-sized snack that tastes just as good as traditional carrot cake without any of the guilt. These energy balls are produced with nutritious, natural ingredients that deliver you a rapid energy boost whether you're on the road, need a lunchtime pick-me-up, or want a treat after your workout. They're ideal for satisfying your sweet tooth without sacrificing your health.

Carrot Cake Energy Balls are unique because of the way they combine flavors and textures. As in classic carrot cake, they have the sweetness of carrots combined with the cozy warmth of nutmeg and cinnamon. Carrot shreds give these snacks a natural sweetness boost, as well as a healthy amount of fiber, antioxidants, and vitamin A, making them both wholesome and delicious.

For vegan, gluten-free, and devoid of refined sugars, these carrot cake energy balls are a fantastic choice for anyone trying to follow a better diet without sacrificing flavor. They are also a wise choice for sustaining energy levels throughout the day due to their blend of natural carbohydrates, fiber, protein, and healthy fats.

They're also ideal for meal preparation. When you need a quick snack, you may prepare a batch ahead of time, put them in the refrigerator, and then grab a couple. They are a handy choice for lunchboxes, office snacks, or post-exercise nutrition because they carry nicely as well.

Ingredients

1 cup of dates with pits

1/4 cup of traditional rolled oats

Chopped pecans, ¼ cup

1/2 a cup of chia seeds

2 medium carrots, almost 4 ounces in total, cut finely

1 tsp vanilla essence

1/2 teaspoon of ground cinnamon

1/2 teaspoon of ground ginger

1/2 teaspoon of ground turmeric

1/2 teaspoon of salt

1 dash of black pepper

In conclusion, Carrot Cake Energy Balls are a tasty and wholesome way to savor carrot cake flavors without having to use extra sugar, wheat, or oil. Rich in the nutritious qualities of carrots, almonds, and dates, these treats are gratifying and guilt-free, suitable for any time of day. These energy balls are the ideal choice whether you're searching for a healthy dessert substitute or a snack that will increase your energy!

CHAPTER 8:

Rice, Grains, and Pasta

Couscous

Originating in North Africa, couscous is a staple cuisine that is extensively consumed around the world. It is composed of small, granular pieces of steamed or crushed wheat or barley. Rolling wet crushed wheat or barley into small, granular shapes and heating or steaming them are the preparatory steps.

Originating in North Africa, couscous is a versatile and light dish that has become a mainstay in many Mediterranean diets. Recognized for its rapid cooking period and versatility, couscous can function as an ideal foundation for an array of dishes, absorbing the tastes of whatever it is combined with.

Though it's frequently mistaken for a grain, couscous is actually a type of pasta made primarily of microscopic semolina wheat granules. These tiny, fluffy grains can be steamed or soaked in hot water to cook them very quickly—usually in a matter of minutes. Because of this, couscous is a quick and easy option for people who want to cook a healthy supper.

There are various varieties of couscous; the most popular is Moroccan couscous, which is the smallest version that cooks the quickest. With its larger, rounder granules, Israeli couscous (also known as pearl couscous) has a somewhat chewier texture and requires a little more cooking time. The largest of the three, Lebanese couscous, has an even more significant bite.

In terms of nutrition, couscous is a fantastic source of carbs that release energy gradually. Additionally, it has a tiny quantity of fiber and protein. Couscous is a vital supplement to a balanced diet even though it lacks the protein content of other grains like quinoa. Its nutritional value can be increased by pairing it with vegetables, lentils, or lean proteins.

The texture of couscous is little gritty and it has a mild flavor. It can be used with sauces, meats, or vegetables and acts as a flexible foundation for many different recipes. Couscous is a staple food in Middle Eastern and North African cuisines, traditionally served with tagines, stews, and other hearty meals. It is frequently served as a side dish or included in salads. The versatility of couscous to absorb the tastes of the dishes it is paired with and its ease of preparation are two of its greatest qualities.

A delightful and light side dish that goes well with roasted vegetables, grilled chicken, or seafood is made when couscous is served with a simple drizzle of olive oil, a squeeze of lemon, and a handful of fresh herbs like parsley or mint. To add more complexity to the flavor, you can also mix in nuts like almonds or pine nuts, dried fruits like raisins or apricots, and spices like cumin, coriander, or cinnamon. Couscous can also be a great way to serve heartier meals; its light texture balances out the deep, robust flavors of these stews, making it a satisfying but not overwhelming base.

Ingredients

1¾ cups water or low-sodium vegetable or chicken broth

1 tablespoon unsalted butter and ½ teaspoon salt

1 tablespoon of pure olive oil

10 ounces, or 1½ cups quick couscous

Instruction

1 Bring water or broth to a boil.

Fill a saucepan with one cup of broth (or water). Add a tiny bit of kosher salt and a tiny drizzle of extra virgin olive oil. Heat up some water to a boil.

2. Use extra virgin olive oil to toast the couscous.

Although it's optional, this step can significantly impact the flavor that is imparted. In a nonstick skillet, heat one to two tablespoons of extra virgin olive oil. Using a wooden spoon, add the raw couscous and stir regularly. The goal is for the couscous to turn a gorgeous golden brown (make sure to pay close attention to this; it will happen quickly).

3. Boil the couscous in water.

In the boiling water, toss the couscous. Remove the sauce pan from the stove or immediately turn off the heat while it's covered. After the couscous has absorbed all of the water, let it remain undisturbed for approximately ten minutes. Take a fork and uncover and fluff. To suit your tastes, add or subtract salt.

4. Not required. For taste, add some herbs and spices.

At this stage, you can serve your couscous plain. Alternatively, feel free to add some fresh herbs and your preferred amount of seasoning. I also added chopped parsley, dill, and green onions, along with a sprinkle of ground cumin. A few minced garlic cloves that have been sautéed in extra virgin olive oil were also added.

After adding your preferred flavorings, give the couscous one more toss to mix it all together before transferring it to a serving tray. Have fun!

THE MEDITERRANEAN DIET COOKBOOK FOR BEGINNERS

Rice

One of the most popular basic foods in the world, rice is a key component of Mediterranean cooking. It is a culinary need because of its adaptability, nutritious content, and capacity to enhance a wide range of recipes, particularly when experimenting with Mediterranean flavors.

Although there are many different kinds of rice, long-grain, medium-grain, and short-grain rice are the most often used variations in Mediterranean cuisine. Every one of these sorts has distinct qualities and functions best in various kinds of recipes.

Long-grain rice, such as basmati or jasmine, is frequently used for Mediterranean recipes because of its fragrant aroma and light, fluffy texture. These kinds work well as a side dish for grilled meats and shellfish, or as an ingredient in pilafs and stuffed vegetables. When cooked, long-grain rice remains distinct and fluffy.

Medium-grain rice, such as arborio or paella rice, is slightly plumper and tends to become creamier when cooked. The star of traditional Mediterranean meals like risotto or paella is the rice, which takes on robust tastes and produces a velvety, rich texture. Arborio rice is particularly renowned for its capacity to release starch after cooking, which eliminates the need for cream and gives risotto its creamy quality.

Although it is not as frequently used in Mediterranean cookery, short-grain rice, like sushi rice, is present in several local recipes. Because of its stickier texture, this rice is ideal for dishes that call for a more cohesive, almost sticky feel.In terms of nutrients, rice is a rich source of carbs, which are necessary for energy production. Compared to white rice, brown rice is a healthier option since it is higher in fiber, B vitamins, and minerals like selenium and magnesium. White rice is still a popular option because of its mild flavor and light texture, even though it is frequently more refined and deficient in some of these elements.

Because of its remarkable versatility and ability to take on the flavors of the foods it is combined with, rice is a staple in many Mediterranean recipes. Rice pilaf is a traditional example, in which the rice is cooked in broth to add flavor after being sautéed in olive oil and aromatic herbs. It frequently serves as an accompaniment to stews made with vegetables, grilled seafood, or roasted meats.

Ingredients

1 cup of white rice (jasmine or basmati)

2 cups of water

Salt

Instructions

1. Fill a medium pot with rice and water; place over high heat and bring to a boil. After it boils, reduce the heat to a simmer and cover. To avoid the rice cooking too quickly, make sure it is simmering rather than boiling.
2. Simmer for 15 to 25 minutes (depending on the size and freshness of the rice) or until the water is

completely absorbed and the rice is soft. If there is any extra water, it should be drained off.

3. In order to avoid mushy rice, I like to turn off the heat, take off the cover, fluff the rice with a fork, replace the lid, and let the rice sit for ten minutes. This allows the moisture to redistribute. This rice is excellent with stews, sushi, stir fries, and other dishes!

4. Cool leftovers can be kept in the freezer for up to a month or covered in the fridge for up to six days. Warm it up again in the microwave or on the stovetop with a little water or oil.

In more sophisticated Mediterranean cuisines, such as paella, a rice dish from Spain that blends seafood, poultry, vegetables, and saffron in a single fragrant pan, rice plays a crucial role. The rice turns golden yellow and acquires a deep, savory taste as it absorbs the liquid and saffron.

Risotto is another classic; usually, arborio rice is used, and it's cooked gently with stock, white wine, and occasionally Parmesan cheese. It's rich and creamy, frequently enriched with asparagus, shrimp, or mushrooms.

Serve rice with a variety of Mediterranean salads for a lighter choice, or make a rice salad by combining rice with fresh ingredients like cucumbers, tomatoes, feta cheese, and herbs. Dripping in some olive oil and adding a squeeze of lemon

Grains

Grains provide nourishment and variety, making them an essential part of the Mediterranean diet. These nutrient-dense powerhouses serve as the foundation for many classic recipes, making them tasty and filling dinners.

Because they are whole grains—that is, they preserve the bran, germ, and endosperm of the grain kernel—grains like farro, bulgur, quinoa, and barley are frequently preferred over more processed grains in the Mediterranean region. As a result, they can offer greater fiber, antioxidants, vitamins, and minerals, all of which improve general health.

The simplicity of the Mediterranean grain-growing philosophy is its key. Even though these grains are frequently cooked with only a few ingredients (olive oil, herbs, and occasionally vegetables), their substantial textures and nutty aromas are evident.

1. Farro

Ancient farro has long been a mainstay of Mediterranean cooking, particularly in Italy. Known for its chewy texture and nutty flavor, farro is typically used in salads, soups, and grain bowls. Because to its high fiber, magnesium, and zinc content, farro is an excellent option for heart health and digestion. Even on its own, a straightforward farro salad with fresh tomatoes, cucumbers, parsley, and a drizzle of olive oil can be a filling and pleasant lunch.

2. Bulgur

Another whole grain that's frequently used in Mediterranean cookery is bulgur. This type of cracked wheat cooks rapidly, which makes it a practical choice for meals. It's likely best recognized for its part in tabbouleh, a Lebanese salad that blends bulgur with parsley, mint, tomatoes, lemon juice, and olive oil. With its high fiber and protein content, bulgur is an excellent method to increase your intake of whole grains without having to prepare them for a long period.

3. Quinoa

Despite not coming from a classically Mediterranean background, quinoa has gained popularity due to its full protein profile, which includes all nine necessary amino acids, which makes it a top choice for vegans and vegetarians. Quinoa is a great substitute for rice or couscous because of its fluffy, airy texture and mildly nutty flavor. It is frequently combined with veggies, herbs, and olive oil and served as a side dish or in salads. Because of its adaptability, it goes well with roasted vegetables, chicken, or seafood that has been grilled.

4. Barley Barley is another ancient grain that is great for hearty dishes like Mediterranean-style stews with lamb, tomatoes, and root vegetables. You'll often find barley added to soups like vegetable barley or mushroom barley soup, giving the dishes more substance and a heartier bite. Its chewy texture can withstand slow cooking. Moreover, barley is particularly rich in beta-glucan, a type of fiber that helps lower cholesterol.

5. Grass

Mediterranean cuisine, especially in North Africa, is known for its couscous. Technically speaking, it is a kind of semolina, a wheat product, rather than a grain. Couscous is a quick and simple dinner base because it cooks in a matter of minutes. Mediterranean cuisine frequently serves couscous as an accompaniment to dishes like grilled lamb or chicken tagine, as well as with stews and roasted vegetables. Couscous can be fluffed with olive oil, lemon zest, and fresh herbs for a simple side dish that is light and pleasant.

6. Unfreekeh

Another ancient grain that is becoming more and more well-liked is freekeh, which has a high protein and fiber content. It's prepared from green wheat that's picked early, roasted, and then rubbed to form a firm, chewy grain. Freekeh pairs well with roasted meats and tastes great in salads, pilafs, and other prepared dishes. It has a hint of smoke to it. It's an excellent complement to a balanced diet because it's especially abundant in calcium and iron.

The Significance of Grains in a Mediterranean Diet

The Mediterranean diet is based mostly on whole grains for a number of reasons. They include a lot of complex carbs, which provide you energy all day long. Whole grains also help manage blood sugar, reduce the risk of heart disease, and support good digestion. You may guarantee that your diet has a broad range of nutrients, such as fiber, magnesium, and B vitamins, by including a variety of grains.

Grain adaptability is another reason why Mediterranean cuisine values grains so highly. Grains make a filling base for meals, whether they are warm in a pilaf, cold in a grain salad, or added to soups and stews. Serving them with crisp veggies, low-fat foods like olive oil, and lean meats like chicken or fish mixing good fats such as olive oil makes balanced, nutritious meals that are as delicious as they are wholesome.

Additionally, grains take well to a variety of flavors and seasonings. A simple squeeze of lemon, a sprinkling of feta cheese, or a few herbs may add color and flavor to a bowl of basic grains. Grain dishes can be elevated above mere sides by adding textures and flavors from fruits, nuts, seeds, and veggies.

Ways to Cook Mediterranean Grains

It's critical to season grains well in advance of cooking. Flavor depth can be achieved by substituting broth for water. Before adding liquid, don't be afraid to briefly toast the grains in a small amount of olive oil. This brings out their inherent nuttiness.

Last but not least, grains can be prepared in large quantities and kept chilled for easy dinners all week long. A portion of precooked quinoa or farro can be added to soups for extra heartiness or used as the foundation for grain bowls and lunch salads.

To sum up, grains are an essential component of the Mediterranean diet and serve as a tasty and nutritious base for a wide variety of dishes. Grain offers a wealth of taste, texture, and health benefits, whether you're having a light quinoa salad, a deep barley stew, or a straightforward bulgur tabbouleh.

Lemon Rice

A bright, rich, and fragrant dish that is both cozy and refreshing is lemon rice. This is a traditional South Indian dish that combines the earthiness of rice with the tanginess of fresh lemon juice, complemented with a few crunchy ingredients and spices. It's a simple yet lovely method to enhance regular rice into something genuinely spectacular.

Rice that has been cooked in water infused with lemon juice and topped with a slice or wedge of fresh lemon are known as lemon rice.

Health Benefits of Lemon Rice

Everyone can enjoy lemon rice because it has been demonstrated to have several health advantages.

-It is a fantastic source of complex carbs and is high in vitamin C, both of which support healthy weight maintenance.

- Rice is a low-glycemic food. Those who are attempting to

reduce their weight or manage their blood sugar levels would benefit from this.

- Rice is an excellent source of vitamins, fiber, and minerals. It has been demonstrated to help prevent heart disease and decrease cholesterol levels.

- Lastly, antioxidants found in rice can help prevent cell damage and lower the chance of developing certain chronic diseases.

What Is Unique About Lemon Rice?

The goal of lemon rice is to balance the flavors and textures of the rice, not just add lemon to it after it's cooked. Fresh lemon juice and zest give the rice's nutty flavor a bright, acidic brightness that goes well with it. Warming spices like curry leaves, mustard seeds, and turmeric combine with a delicious crunch from peanuts or cashews. Garnish with chopped cilantro or chopped green chilies for a little heat and freshness.

Instruction.

Well, lemon rice will be a terrific option if you're tired of making and eating gravies all day and want to try something fresh and easy. I'll walk you through the process here so you can quickly and easily create delicious lemon rice.

1. Whether it's an induction stove or a gas hob, place a pan on your cooktop.
2. Add two teaspoons of oil and allow to warm for a while.
3. Add ½ tablespoon of Chana dal (split chickpeas), ½ tablespoon of mustard, and cook it thoroughly for one minute.
4. Next, add the peanuts and toast them thoroughly until they turn brown.
5. After everything has been well fried, add two to three whole red chilies and sauté everything again until it is not charred.
6. Let's now add chopped ginger and curry leaves to your dish to enhance its aroma.
7. After completing the aforementioned steps, gently sauté everything for nearly a minute.
8. Let's now add half a tablespoon of turmeric powder, which will give the rice the necessary color, and thoroughly combine it.
9. Now add the previously boiled and kept rice, stir it into the prepared components, and give it a good sauté.
10. To achieve the flavor of the lemon, add 1 ½ tablespoon of lemon juice and a touch of salt according to the amount of rice you added.
11. After adding everything, give it a good stir for about a minute, then turn off the stove.
12. and now let's divide it into a bowl, add some coriander leaves to the top, and taste it to experience the delicious flavor of homemade lemon rice.

Ingredients

2 tablespoons of mustard oil or vegetable oil

1 yellow onion, cut into half-moons

1 minced garlic clove

1 tablespoon black mustard seed

1 tsp cumin seeds

2 tsp of turmeric

2 cups of basmati rice

4 cups water

4 tsp freshly squeezed lemon juice

2 tablespoons of chopped chives

When to Savor Rice with Lemon

Rice with lemon is ideal for any situation. Its flavourful and vivid combination makes it a unique side dish for parties, yet it's light enough for a quick weeknight dinner. For additional flavor levels, it goes well with yogurt-based dips like raita, grilled veggies, or Indian-style pickles.

This dish is excellent for meal prep as well. Make a big amount ahead of time and keep it chilled for a few days; just warm it up right before serving. As it rests, the flavors tend to intensify, making leftovers even more flavourful.

Pasta and Couscous Recipes

Pasta and couscous recipes are staples in many cultures across the world because they are so flavourful, textural, and versatile. You can make them as simple or as complex as you choose, from weeknight dinners to more intricate concoctions fit for special occasions.

Wheat is an element that both pasta and couscous have in common, despite differences in size, shape, and preparation. They are both adored for being versatile enough to hold a wide range of ingredients, including fresh veggies, protein, and rich sauces. Moreover, they adjust nicely to various diets, be it gluten-free, healthful, or substantial.

Pasta Recipes

Pasta is available in a variety of shapes, including spaghetti, penne, fusilli, farfalle, and others, each of which is intended to handle sauces differently. Pasta offers countless options for preparation, whether you're making a simple linguine with garlic and olive oil, a decadent carbonara, or a lasagna filled with vegetables. Here are some noteworthy pasta meal suggestions:

A classic Italian recipe that emphasizes the beauty of simple ingredients is spaghetti aglio e olio. Spaghetti strands are coated in olive oil, garlic, and chili flakes; a pinch of Parmesan or Pecorino cheese adds a salty touch.

Pesto Pasta: A bright green pesto made with fresh basil, pine nuts, garlic, and olive oil gives any pasta a nutty, herbaceous taste. Toss with your preferred pasta form for an easy, nourishing meal.

Baked Ziti: Ziti pasta, marinara sauce, ricotta cheese, and mozzarella are baked till golden and bubbling in this hearty baked pasta dish. It embodies the best of hearty, casual Italian-American cuisine.

Seafood Linguine: A sophisticated, light pasta meal with a blast of oceanic tastes is made with fresh seafood, such as shrimp, mussels, and clams, tossed with linguine in a white wine and garlic sauce.

Vegetable Primavera: This bright and refreshing pasta dish is made with a lot of sautéed seasonal vegetables mixed in a light garlic sauce. It's a fantastic way to get your recommended daily intake of vegetables without compromising flavor.

Couscous Recipes

The microscopic durum wheat granule known as couscous is a mainstay in Middle Eastern and North African cooking, but pasta is more prevalent in Italian and Western cuisines. Recipes using couscous are frequently fluffy, light, and full of veggies, spices, and occasionally meat or shellfish. Here are some suggestions for couscous dishes:

Moroccan Couscous: Packed with warming spices like cumin, cinnamon, and turmeric, this recipe is one of the most popular ways to prepare couscous. It is frequently served with slow-cooked meats like chicken or lamb, along with dried fruits like raisins or apricots, and toasted almonds as a garnish.

Couscous Salad: During the summer, couscous salads are light and pleasant. Tossed with chopped veggies like cucumbers, tomatoes, and red onions, fresh herbs like parsley and mint, and olive oil and lemon juice, it's a flavourful and filling dish.

Couscous with Roasted Vegetables: Coriander, cumin, and bell peppers are added to couscous along with roasted carrots, bell peppers, zucchini, and eggplant. This is a delicious side dish that goes well as a vegetarian main course or with grilled meats.

Bell peppers are hollowed out, filled with couscous, cheese, and sautéed veggies, and baked until soft. This recipe is known as couscous-stuffed peppers. This results in a vivid, colourful dinner that is both aesthetically pleasing and appetizing.

With grilled chicken, fresh herbs, and a lemon vinaigrette, Israeli couscous—also referred to as pearl couscous because of its larger, rounder size—has a chewier texture. This hearty, satisfying dish is ideal for lunch or dinner.

The nutritional benefits of both pasta and couscous are as follows: pasta is a good source of carbohydrates, which the body uses as fuel; whole grain versions of these can offer more fiber, which helps with digestion and heart health; couscous can also be a great source of essential vitamins and protein, especially when combined with legumes and vegetables; pasta dishes can be customized to meet your dietary needs.

Flexibility and Combinations

Because of their adaptability, couscous and pasta go well with a wide range of dishes. Given its versatility, pasta is a great partner for light, olive oil-based recipes, creamy sauces, and tomato-based sauces. Conversely, couscous tastes best when paired with herbs, spices, and dried fruits.

These recipes can be made as healthy or as decadent as you like. For a heartier supper, add seafood, pork, or plant-based proteins; for a lighter meal, just add veggies and herbs. Because they both keep and reheat well, they are also excellent for meal prep.

CHAPTER 9:

Beans, Legumes, and Vegetable Mains

Baked Vegetable Pasta

This vegetable spaghetti bake is a delicious, satisfying comfort food that even meat eaters will love.

One of those hearty, warming recipes that combines the freshness of fresh veggies with rich flavors is baked vegetable pasta. Whether you're searching for a wholesome, easy-to-make dinner for a get-together, or a simple, fulfilling supper for your family, this is the ideal choice.

What Is Unique About Baked Vegetable Pasta?

The comforting familiarity of pasta is combined with the nutritional benefits of a variety of veggies in this recipe. Its adaptability is what makes it so beautiful; you can alter the veggies to suit your tastes, the produce that's in season, or just what's in your refrigerator. First, roasting or sautéing the vegetables brings out their inherent sweetness, which complements the cheese and sauce so well.

Ingredients

Around 400 g (14 oz) of dried pasta shapes I used: rigatoni;

1 tbsp vegetable oil;

1 large red onion,

peeled and chopped into wedges;

 1 red bell pepper,

de-seeded and chopped into large chunks;

1 yellow bell pepper,

de-seeded and chopped into large chunks;

1 large or 2 small courgettes,

chopped into chunks;

1 tbsp tomato puree paste for US;

2 minced cloves of garlic;

1/2 teaspoon dried thyme 2 x 400 g (2 x 14 oz)

Chopped tomatoes in a can 120 ml (1/2 cup)

Triple cream (thick) ▪▪100 g (3 tightly packed cups)

100 g (1 cup) of fresh baby spinach Grated strong cheddar cheese,

100 g (1 cup) grated mozzarella, a small handful of finely shredded parsley

Instruction

1. Set the oven's temperature to 190°C (375°F) (fan).

Bring a big pan of water to a boil and cook the pasta for one minute less than the package suggests. Empty.

14 ounces (400 g) of dried pasta shapes

2. Heat the oil in a big frying pan over medium heat while the pasta cooks. Cook the red onion for three to four minutes, or until it begins to soften.

One large red onion and one tablespoon of vegetable oil

3. Add the tomato puree, oregano, thyme, garlic, sliced peppers, courgette, and salt and pepper. Cook, stirring, for

two to three minutes.

Two cloves of garlic, one tablespoon tomato puree, one red bell pepper, one yellow bell pepper, one large or two tiny courgettes, 1/4 teaspoon salt, 1/4 teaspoon pepper, ½ teaspoon dried oregano, and ½ teaspoon dried thyme

4. Add the cream and canned tomatoes and stir until a light bubble forms.

100 g (3 packed cups) of fresh baby spinach, 120 ml (1/2 cup) of double (heavy) cream, and two 400 g (2 x 14 oz) of canned chopped tomatoes

5. After the pasta has cooked, drain it and combine it with the spinach and sauce. Transfer to a large baking dish after stirring everything together.

6. Add the mozzarella and cheddar on top, then bake for 20 to 25 minutes, or until the cheese is golden brown.

100 g (1 cup) mozzarella and 100 g (1 cup) strong cheddar cheese

7. Before serving, remove from the oven and sprinkle with the parsley.

Parsley in a little bunch.

Sicilian Caponata

Pronounced ka·puh·naa·tuh, caponata Sicilian is a vegetarian eggplant salad—more like a relish, actually—made of eggplant, onions, bell pepper, celery, and tomatoes with briny olives and capers.

There are several variations of this delicious eggplant salad, most of which are flavored with vinegar. Some recipes call for raisins, which I adore and use in this caponata recipe. Many recipes call for brown sugar to add a little sweetness, but I use a small amount of honey, which is adequate considering the raisins.

Caponata: What is it?

Caponata is fundamentally a sweet and sour eggplant-based dish that is usually prepared with a variety of vegetables, including tomatoes, onions, celery, and olives. For a bright, briny kick, capers and a splash of vinegar are added at the end. The agrodolce flavor profile of caponata, which is different from many Sicilian meals in its balance of sweet and sour, is what really sets it apart.

A wonderful celebration of fresh, in-season veggies with robust Mediterranean tastes, Sicilian caponata is a colourful, savory dish that perfectly embodies Sicilian cuisine. Although it is typically served as an appetizer or side dish, its adaptability allows it to easily take center stage in your meal.

Ingredients

One huge eggplant About 1 ¼ pounds, divided into 1-inch cubes

☐Extra virgin olive oil and kosher salt I used Private Reserve EVOO,

one chopped yellow onion,

one red bell pepper that had been cored and diced,

two thinly sliced celery stalks, black pepper,

one cup of crushed tomatoes,

two tablespoons of capers,

one cup of pitted green olives, coarsely chopped pitted green olives,

one cup of raisins, two teaspoons of honey, or more to taste.

One bay leaf, 1/4 cup red wine vinegar,

¼ to ½ teaspoon crushed red pepper flakes,

☐¼ cup dry white wine,

2 tablespoons chopped fresh parsley,

2 tablespoons chopped fresh mint

Instruction

1. Preheat the oven to 400°F.
2. While you prepare the other ingredients, season the eggplant cubes with salt. If you have the time, let them sit in a colander for 20 to 30 minutes to sweat out the bitterness. Use a paper towel to pat dry.
3. Spread a substantial amount of extra virgin olive oil (about 3 tablespoons) over the seasoned eggplant cubes on a sheet pan and toss to coat. The eggplant should be browned after 25 to 30 minutes of roasting in a preheated oven.
4. In a large skillet, heat 2 tablespoons of extra virgin olive oil. Add the bell pepper, celery, and onions. Add a dash of black pepper and kosher salt for seasoning. Cook, tossing, for 5 to 7 minutes.
5. Add the bay leaf, crushed pepper flakes, tomatoes, capers, olives, raisins, and honey.
6. Add the white wine and vinegar. Mix to blend. For ten minutes, simmer over medium-low heat.
7. Add the roasted eggplant and simmer in the sauce for an additional two to three minutes. Add some fresh mint and parsley at the end.

Mushroom Chickpea Tagine

A hearty, satisfying, and tasty dish that highlights the diversity of Moroccan cooking is Mushroom Chickpea Tagine. This plant-based version of the classic tagine showcases the richness of spices, substantial veggies, and the amazing adaptability of chickpeas, making it the ideal dish for anybody seeking a filling and fragrant supper.

The term "tagine" refers to both the traditional North African stew and the cone-shaped clay pot used to cook it. A tagine pot's slow cooking method lets the contents permeate and steam together, producing a deliciously aromatic and tender dish. Although this dish is typically made with meat, vegetarian variations, such as this Mushroom Chickpea Tagine, are just as tasty because of the extensive use of spices and plant-based ingredients.

Instructions

After trimming the leek's roots and top 3 cm, cut it in half and rinse it to remove any remaining dirt. Slice it thinly. Place the leek and ½ tablespoon of olive oil in a medium-sized pan over medium heat. Add a dash of salt and pepper for seasoning.

1. Stirring often, fry the leek for 6 minutes, or until it has softened and begun to brown.

2. Tear the mushrooms into little pieces in the meanwhile. Chop the apricots roughly. Rinse the chickpeas after draining. Fill your kettle and bring it to a boil.

3. Add the mushrooms to the softened leek and cook, turning frequently, for 5 minutes, or until the mushrooms seem moist. Fill your kettle and bring it to a boil in the meanwhile.

4. Put the chickpeas and dried apricots in the pan. Add ½ to 1 tsp harissa paste (use as much or as little as you like; it's hot). Add 2 tsp ras el hanout and 2 tsp honey (save the remainder for later); you may always start with a small amount and add more at the end. Add the chopped tomatoes and stir. Cover, bring to a boil, reduce the heat, and simmer for 10 minutes, or until the chickpeas are cooked and the mixture has slightly thickened.

5. Transfer the couscous to a heatproof basin while the tagine simmers. Add 150 milliliters of boiling water. Use a fork to swirl, place a plate over the bowl, and leave for ten minutes. The water will be absorbed by the couscous.

6. If you think the tagine needs more salt, pepper, honey, or harissa, taste it and add more. Using a fork, fluff the couscous and distribute it between two bowls or plates that are heated. Place the tagine on top, then serve.

A Tasty Plant-Based Treat: Mushroom Chickpea Tagine is quite healthy in addition to being flavourful. Mushrooms supply vital vitamins and minerals, while chickpeas offer plant-based protein. This recipe is a fantastic choice for people who are on a plant-based or healthy eating regimen because it is naturally vegan, gluten-free, and high in fiber.

Ideal for Preparing Meals

As the tagine sits, the flavors intensify, which is one of its finest features. This is simple to prepare ahead of time and may be enjoyed over a few days. Additionally, you can batch cook and keep leftovers for a quick and filling supper at a later time because it is freezer-friendly.

Greek Chickpeas with Potato and Spinach

Showcasing the finest of Mediterranean cuisine, Greek Chickpeas with Potato and Spinach is a hearty, nutrient-rich dish. It's a straightforward yet tasty blend of soft potatoes, colourful spinach, and nourishing chickpeas, all seasoned with traditional Greek spices. This dish has a great blend of flavors and textures, making it a great choice for a healthy vegetarian meal or as a side dish to go with grilled meats or fish.

It only takes ten basic ingredients, most of which you may find in your cupboard, to make this lemony chickpea soup, and half of the potato and chickpea base is pureed to make it extra creamy and filling.

Instruction.

1. Turn up the heat to medium in a big pot with a hefty bottom. Add the olive oil to the saucepan and stir it around once it's heated. To the pot, add the onions. Sauté them for 6 to 7 minutes, stirring regularly, until they are extremely soft and completely transparent. Reduce the heat if they start to brown.

2. Fill the saucepan with the celery and carrot. For around five minutes, sauté the celery with the onions, turning periodically, until it is just beginning to soften around the edges. Add salt and pepper to the vegetables.

3. Stir the lemon zest, garlic, chilies, and thyme into the pot. Sauté for approximately one minute, or until the lemon and garlic are extremely aromatic.

4. Season with salt and pepper once more after adding the potatoes and chickpeas to the pot. Stir everything around. Next, fill the pot with the vegetable stock. After giving the soup one last toss, cover it.

5. After bringing the soup to a boil, reduce the heat so that it simmers. To allow some steam to escape, place the pot's cover askew. Continue to boil for another 15 minutes or until the potatoes are extremely soft.

6. Gently pour half of the soup into an upright blender with a vent. Put this mixture in the blender on high and blend until it's smooth. Return the soup's pureed portion to the pot and stir. Stir in the baby spinach after adding it to the pot again.

Stir again after adding the lemon juice when the spinach has wilted. Make any necessary adjustments to the soup's seasoning by adding extra lemon, salt, pepper, chile, etc.

7. Top the heated soup with additional black pepper and olive oil

drizzles.

Ingredients

- 1 medium yellow onion, thinly sliced;
- 2 tablespoons olive oil
- 1 medium carrot, cut into little pieces
- 1 stick of small-diced celery
- 3 minced garlic cloves
- sea salt and ground black pepper, to taste
- 1 tablespoon chopped fresh thyme leaves;

1 teaspoon lemon zest;

½ teaspoon crushed chilies or chile flakes, or to taste

- 4 cups vegetable stock;

4 cups baby spinach, unpackaged;

1 teaspoon lemon juice, plus additional (see note);

3 medium new potatoes, cut into ¾-inch cubes (about 3 cups diced potato);

1 ½ cups cooked chickpeas, drained and rinsed if using canned;

Nutritional Benefits

This dish is nutrient-dense in addition to being delicious:

• Chickpeas boost digestion and energy levels by offering plant-based protein, fiber, and vital vitamins like iron and folate.

• Spinach is rich in iron and antioxidants, which support immune function and general health; potatoes provide potassium and vitamin C, which support heart health and a balanced diet.

• Healthy fats, vitamins, and a refreshing finish are added by the olive oil, lemon, and fresh herbs, making this dish as filling as it is nutritious.

A Taste of Greece at Home

A great example of the Mediterranean diet, which emphasizes complete, plant-based foods and healthy fats, is Greek Chickpeas with Potato and Spinach. It's a hearty, filling recipe that combines basic ingredients with bold tastes, making it ideal for a weeknight supper or a visually striking dish to serve to visitors.

Lebanese Mujadara

Rice, lentils, and caramelized onions combine to make the filling and hearty Lebanese meal known as mujadara. A mainstay of Middle Eastern and Lebanese cooking, it is praised for its nutritious value, earthy flavors, and simplicity. The beauty of mujadara is found in its simple ingredients, which combine to make a very filling dish. This recipe is proof that healthy, traditional foods can be tasty and nutritious, whether they are eaten as a side dish or as a vegetarian main course.

Probably one of my top ten favorite foods in the world is mujadara. I believe that speaks something because Nutter Butter cookies are on that list.

In my opinion, Mujadara is the closest thing to a food that was made by God. Lentils and brown rice combine to provide a complete protein that contains all of the important amino acids present in meat. Along with the onions, the parsley offers some dark greens, adding a significant amount of vegetable nutrients to the dish. In addition, there is some fruit included to ensure that all four food groups are satisfied, assuming you are cool enough to consume the lemon garnish. Even some healthy fat is provided by the olive oil that is used to caramelize the onions.

To be honest, it seems as though whoever created the human body and identified the nutrients it needed also put Mujadara on Earth to meet those needs.

It is this traditional mujadara recipe that I think of as my backup go-to in the kitchen. It's one of those recipes where the finished product is better than the parts. The three primary components of Lebanese mujadara are rice, lentils, and onions. These straightforward ingredients work together so well, and the texture of the delicate grains with the deeply caramelized and fried onions is amazing!

Ingredients

Lentils: For this recipe, use large brown whole lentils. They add the nicest texture to the mujadara, and the recipe's color is a defining feature.

For mujadara, you can use almost any kind of rice, but I like to use white long-grain rice because it's the traditional method and provides the nicest texture. The cooking time will need to be increased if you're using brown rice. You can also substitute cracked wheat or bulgur for the rice.

Oil and onions: While the mujadara cooks, the sliced onions are pan-fried until crispy and then placed on paper towels. They crisp up while they sit and make a tasty topping.

Seasonings: salt to taste and cumin

Instruction.

1. **Make use of the appropriate lentils**. The store has a wide variety of lentils. I have tested a variety of brown and green lentils, and most of them would work nicely in this recipe. However, don't use orange or red lentils. They will work better in a mushy consistency for the mujadara (mudardara) recipe because of their softer texture.

2. **Pay close attention to how the lentils are cooking**. Depending on the kind, cooking times for lentils might vary, much like for

many other beans. They will continue to cook with the rice, so follow the package's directions and cook them al dente first.

3. **Cook the onions with assurance**. Although cooking two large onions in ½ cup of oil while turning frequently may seem like a lengthy time, nothing should burn. The amount of oil and the moisture in the onion help to crisp and caramelize them. A fantastic approach to make use of your time when working on such a hands-on element of the recipe is to do this while the rice and lentils cook in a different pot.

4. **Prepare the lentils and rice independently**. I prefer to cook everything at once to save time and not have to wash an additional pot. On the other hand, you can cook the lentils in a separate pot and the rice in a separate pot, then mix them together. As a result, the presentation is improved so I do it for guests sometimes

A Classic Comfort Food

The quintessential comfort food is Lebanese Mujadara, a hearty, rustic dish. It is a staple in Lebanese homes and is frequently eaten during the week or as a dish to share with family and friends. For home cooks, it's easy preparation and inexpensive components make it a useful but delectable choice.

Mujadara's adaptability is what really sets it apart. This recipe is a staple that everyone will like, whether you're preparing meals for the week or cooking for a big family get-together. Additionally, because the flavors have had more time to develop and meld, it tastes even better the next day.

CHAPTER 10:

Vegetables

Roasted Vegetable Dishes

Vegetable dishes that are roasted are the pinnacle of easy yet delicious cooking. Roasting veggies releases richer, caramelized tastes that elevate ordinary items to exceptional heights. Vegetables' inherent sweetness is enhanced by roasting, which also gives them a delicate texture on the inside and a little crunch on the surface.

A Mediterranean-inspired Roasted Chicken and Vegetable Couscous is a tasty roasted vegetable dish that combines chicken, rice, and/or pasta.

Why Roast the Vegetable?

Flavor: The sugars in vegetables caramelize on the high heat of the oven, producing rich, complex flavors; even finicky eaters frequently find themselves enjoying vegetables they wouldn't normally eat because roasting brings out their natural flavor. Ease of use: Simply toss your vegetables with olive oil, season them, and put them in the oven; it's a hands-off method that allows you to concentrate on other aspects of your meal; Versatility: You can roast nearly any vegetable, including carrots, zucchini, Brussels sprouts, sweet potatoes, bell peppers, cauliflower, and more; you can even combine different vegetables for a bright, colourful medley; Health Benefits: Roasting preserves more nutrients than boiling or steaming; when done with healthy fats like olive oil,It transforms vegetables into a nutritious, healthful side dish or main course.

Ingredients.

Boneless and skinless chicken breasts or thighs

Sliced red, yellow, and/or orange bell peppers

Sliced zucchini

- Cherry tomatoes

Sliced red onion

Minced garlic cloves

- Olive oil

Juice from lemons

Dried oregano

Dry thyme

To taste, add salt and black pepper.

- Couscous (or, if desired, rice or pasta)

- Chicken broth (or, if vegetarian, vegetable broth)

Chopped fresh parsley (for garnish)

Instruction

Set the oven temperature to 425°F (220°C).

2. Add the red onion, zucchini, cherry tomatoes, and bell pepper slices to a large mixing bowl.

3. Combine olive oil, lemon juice, minced garlic, dried oregano, dried thyme, salt, and black pepper in a different small bowl to create a marinade for the chicken.

4. Make sure the chicken pieces are thoroughly coated by submerging them in the marinade. If you have more time, marinate the chicken for a few hours, but at least 15 to 20 minutes will improve the flavors.

5. Make the couscous (or rice or pasta) as directed on the package while the chicken marinades. To add more flavor, use chicken broth (or veggie broth) in place of water.

6. Arrange the pieces of marinated chicken evenly on a baking sheet. On the same baking sheet, surround the chicken with the marinated vegetables.

7. In a preheated oven, roast the chicken and veggies for 20 to 25 minutes, or until the chicken is cooked through and the vegetables are soft and have a hint of caramel.

8. Transfer the cooked rice, pasta, or couscous to a serving tray after fluffing it with a fork.

9. Place the roasted chicken and veggies on top of the couscous.

10. To add freshness and a splash of color, garnish the meal with freshly chopped parsley.

Nutritional Benefits

Roasted vegetables are not only tasty but also nutrient-dense. Important vitamins and minerals are preserved by roasting, and fat-soluble vitamins like A, D, E, and K are better absorbed when healthy fats like olive oil are added. Additionally, the high fiber content of vegetables like sweet potatoes, broccoli, and Brussels sprouts supports digestive health and prolongs feelings of fullness.

Experiment with Different Flavors

Although olive oil, salt, and pepper are basic seasonings, you can experiment with other flavors. Try a variety of spice combinations, such as curry powder for an Indian touch, smoked paprika for a touch of smokiness, or za'atar for a Middle Eastern edge. A squeeze of lemon or a drizzle of balsamic vinegar adds a hint of acidity that lifts the meal, while fresh herbs like parsley, thyme, or rosemary can provide brightness.

Easy Vegetable Sides

Easy veggie sides are the ideal choice if you're searching for a quick and wholesome way to go with your meal. They are adaptable enough to go well with a variety of cuisines, provide vital nutrients, and give any dish a healthy balance. Vegetable sides are also usually easy to prepare, which makes them perfect for easy entertaining or hectic weeknights.

Carrots are wonderfully sautéed. Carrots should be peeled and sliced. Start them in a large amount of cold water with a spoonful of salt added. After bringing to a boil, simmer until barely soft. Chop one large scallion while the carrots are boiling. Once carrots are cooked, drain and pat dry with a paper towel. Melt a tablespoon of butter in a nonstick sauté pan, then add the minced scallions. Add the carrots and stir until they become transparent. Add a little light cream after sautéing the carrots for a few minutes to warm them through. Cook slowly until the cream has been absorbed. (It's hard to tell how much because it depends on how old the carrots are, the quantity you're preparing, and the desired level of creaminess. Add another tablespoon of butter when they have absorbed the cream, season with salt and freshly ground black pepper to taste, and garnish with a few nutmeg grates. These are sure to please even the pickiest eaters.

Tips for Creating Quick and Delicious Vegetable Sides

Select Seasonal Vegetables: Vegetables taste more vivid, sweet, and fresh when they are in season. They're also easier to locate at your local market and more reasonably priced. In the colder months, choose winter squash and root vegetables; in the warmer months, choose tomatoes, asparagus, and zucchini.

Keep It Simple: The simplest vegetable sides are frequently the most delectable. The natural flavors of your vegetables can be accentuated without overpowering them with a squeeze of lemon, a dash of salt and pepper, and a drizzle of olive oil.

Employ a Variety of Cooking Techniques: Sautéing, grilling, steaming, and roasting are all rapid ways to enhance the flavor of vegetables. Depending on the vegetable, you can mix and match different techniques or even combine them, such as blanching and then sautéing for a crisp-tender

Use Fresh Herbs and Spices: Add herbs like cilantro, thyme, or parsley to your veggie sides, or add smoked paprika, cumin, or chili flakes to make them more interesting. With little work, herbs and spices give your food a restaurant-caliber flavor by adding depth and complexity.

Sautéed Green Beans with Garlic

A crisp, tangy side dish that goes well with roasted chicken or grilled meats is made by sautéing green beans with garlic and a little lemon juice. Just blanch the green beans first, then cook them in olive oil and garlic until they are just beginning to brown.

2. Carrots Roasted with Thyme and Honey

Toss baby carrots with honey, olive oil, and fresh thyme for a mildly flavourful and sweet alternative. Roast them until they are soft and caramelized at 400°F (200°C). The thyme lends a fragrant herbal aroma, while the honey highlights the carrots' inherent sweetness.

Brussels Sprouts Glazed with Balsamic

When roasted to crispy perfection, Brussels sprouts are a hit with everyone. Roast Brussels sprouts until golden after tossing them with salt, pepper, and olive oil. For a tangy, somewhat sweet contrast, sprinkle some balsamic glaze over the top.

4. Parmesan Crispy Zucchini

Rounds of thinly sliced zucchini tossed with breadcrumbs, Parmesan cheese, and olive oil create a delicious and crispy side dish. Bake or roast them until they are crispy and brown. This goes well with spaghetti or any main course prepared in the Italian style.

5. Garlic and Sautéed Spinach

One of the quickest and healthiest sides you can prepare is a simple sauté of fresh spinach with garlic and olive oil. You'll have a colourful, nutrient-dense side dish in a matter of minutes that goes well with fish, poultry, or you could even put it in your breakfast omelette.

6. Asparagus on the Grill with Lemon Zest

A simple yet sophisticated side dish is grilled asparagus. After tossing the asparagus stalks with salt, pepper, and olive oil, grill them until they are soft and have a little of char. For added taste and brightness, sprinkle Parmesan and lemon zest on top.

7. Turmeric and Roasted Cauliflower

Turmeric adds a warm, earthy taste to roasted cauliflower florets. To add a little heat, add a dash of cayenne and a sprinkle of cumin. Roast the florets until they are crispy and golden. This side goes well with dishes that have an Indian or Middle Eastern flair.

8. Herb-topped mashed potatoes

Small potatoes should be boiled until soft, then gently mashed and roasted until crispy. Sprinkle with fresh herbs and drizzle with olive oil, such as parsley or rosemary. These potatoes are enticing because of their soft cores and crunchy edges.

9. Lemon and Chili Flakes with Broccoli

Broccoli florets can be roasted or steamed, then tossed with a little lemon vinaigrette and a dash of chili flakes for a little heat. Bright and zesty, this recipe is quick and simple and goes well with almost anything.

10. Cilantro and Lime on Grilled Corn

It's difficult to top the smoky sweetness that grilled corn brings when it's in season. Grill the cobs until they are lightly browned after brushing them with a little butter or olive oil. For a cool touch, squeeze fresh lime juice over the top and garnish with chopped cilantro.

Nutritional Benefits

There's more to vegetable sides than merely filling your plate. They supply vital nutrients, such as vitamins, minerals, and fiber. Including a range of veggies in your diet can improve immune function, aid with digestion, and lower your chance of developing chronic illnesses. Additionally, vegetable sides can help you feel full and invigorated because they are high in nutrients and low in calories.

CHAPTER 11:

Fish & Seafood

Greek Mussels with Lemon Rice

Greek Mussels with Lemon Rice is a great option if you're craving a flavourful, light, Mediterranean-inspired dish that combines the fresh taste of mussels with the zesty brightness of lemon rice, resulting in a delightful balance of briny seafood and citrusy, herb-infused rice.

Why Greek Mussels with Lemon Rice?

This dish is a celebration of simple yet bold flavors, with the mussels absorbing all the wonderful aromas while cooking in a fragrant broth of white wine, garlic, and fresh herbs, while the lemon rice adds a refreshing, tangy twist. The result is a light yet filling meal, with the rice serving as a comforting foundation for the delicate mussels.

Ingredients

For the Mussels:

- 2 lbs fresh mussels, cleaned and debearded
- 1/2 cup dry white wine

- 4 cloves garlic, minced
- 1 small onion, finely chopped
- 2 tbsp olive oil
- 1/2 cup chopped fresh parsley
- Juice of 1 lemon
- Salt and pepper to taste

For the Lemon Rice:

- 1 cup long-grain rice (Basmati or Jasmine work well)
- 2 cups vegetable or chicken broth
- Zest and juice of 1 lemon
- 2 tbsp olive oil
- 1 tsp salt
- 1/4 cup fresh dill or parsley, finely chopped

Get the Lemon Rice ready:

Heat the olive oil in a medium saucepan over medium heat. To coat the rice in the oil, add it and stir. Cook until the rice is lightly browned, about 2 minutes.

Add the lemon juice, salt, and broth and bring to a boil. The rice should be soft and cooked through after about 15 minutes of simmering over low heat with a lid on.

When finished, add the lemon zest and fresh parsley or dill for a zesty taste.

Prepare the mussels:

Heat the olive oil in a big skillet or pot over medium heat. Sauté the garlic and chopped onions for two to three minutes, or until they are fragrant and tender.

Add the cleaned mussels after adding the white wine and

bringing to a simmer.

For approximately five to seven minutes, or until all of the mussels have opened, cover the saucepan and allow them to steam. Throw away those that don't open.

Finish the mussels with a hefty handful of chopped parsley, salt, pepper, and a squeeze of fresh lemon juice.

Serving:

Spoon the mussels over a generous amount of lemon rice and serve them straight from their aromatic broth. For added zing, garnish with a lemon wedge and more fresh herbs.

Nutritional Benefits

Mussels are a great option for heart health because they are abundant in omega-3 fatty acids and high-quality protein. Additionally, they supply vital minerals like iron, zinc, and selenium, which boost immunity and general

Greek Mussels with Lemon Rice is a healthy and revitalizing dish that instantly takes you to Greece's sunny beaches. It's a tasty, wholesome, and aesthetically pleasing dish that will wow whether you're preparing it for a family supper or serving it at a get-together with friends. It's also rather easy to make, which makes it a great choice for evening dinners when you want to add a little bit extra.

Spaghetti Vongole

A traditional Italian meal that captures the flavor of the sea right on your plate is spaghetti vongole. This recipe, which is made with fresh clams, garlic, white wine, and a touch of chile, is straightforward but exquisite, showcasing the clams' inherent brininess and the delicate texture of spaghetti. Despite the fact that everyone is free to prepare this dish anyway they like, there are a few things that really irritate me. For this reason, I make it frequently at home rather than ordering it out very often.

Cleaning your clams is the first and most crucial rule. Nothing is more irritating than having clams on your dish covered in sand, even though it could take some time. A single one can spoil an entire batch.

It makes me insane. You can't just spit out the shelves, can you? Therefore, you must carefully extract the small meat from the shell and throw them away. After that, you can begin eating your cold spaghetti. Some claim that the clams are there to demonstrate that clams are used in its creation. Simply use shells to adorn your food. I'll visit the beach if I want to pick shells.

Although I have nothing against the use of tomatoes in this recipe, a too large or juicy tomato detracts from the overall flavor. A common characteristic of spaghetti con le vongole is its creaminess, which is achieved by mixing the clam juice, olive oil, and some of the starchy water your pasta boiled in. That can be ruined by tomatoes, which are known to be watery. "Crime in the kitchen" should be the title of the featured meal.

Why would you add chili pepper to this ideal dish? Before serving, remove the garlic. There's no need to savor it; it tastes fantastic nevertheless. Half of the parsley is used while cooking, and the other half is added right away. Use good wine if you use white wine—there's no need for that.

Ingredients

175 grams of dry spaghetti

2 tablespoons of olive oil

1 big garlic clove

ROLL ALEX

1/2 a teaspoon of chilli flakes

1/2 a cup of white wine

500 grams of fresh clams

1 tiny pinch of fresh parsley and half a lemon

Freshly ground black pepper and sea salt

Instruction

Get your supplies and ingredients ready. You'll need a lidded deep pot and another saucepan for the pasta. Prepare a basin for the broth, a bowl for the shells, and a colander in the sink.

Assemble your ingredients. Rinse the clams under cool running water, crush the garlic, and slice the parsley. Throw away those that have broken shells. All you have to do is tap any open clams on a surface. Discard it if it doesn't close.

Pour salted water into the pasta pan and come to a boil.

Add 1 tablespoon of olive oil and the garlic to the other pan, the one with the lid. Once the garlic is sizzling, swirl it to keep it from sticking. Next, add the wine, clams, and chilli flakes. After bringing to a boil, place a lid on it and let it steam for five minutes.

In the meantime, prepare the spaghetti as directed on the package. Complete all necessary tasks, such as setting the table and cleaning up.

Strain the liquid into one of the extra dishes when the clams have cooked and opened. Half of the clams should have their meat removed, and the empty shells should be thrown in the other bowl. Verify again that every clam has opened.

The pasta should be done by now, so strain it thoroughly in a colander. Add the spaghetti, clam broth, and naked clams (clams without shells) back to the same pan. Bring to a simmer and season with salt, pepper, lemon juice, and the remaining 1 tablespoon of olive oil.

Serve with more lemon after adding the chopped parsley and the clams in their shells.

The quintessential Italian dish is spaghetti vongole, which is straightforward, flavourful, and fresh. When prepared correctly, this dish—which depends on high-quality ingredients—makes for a memorable culinary experience. Spaghetti Vongole is the ideal option whether you want to relive an Italian seaside memory or simply want to have a light, seafood-focused meal. This recipe, which is simple to prepare but has a sophisticated flavor, can quickly become a mainstay in your culinary arsenal.

Skate Piccata

An elegant, flavourful seafood dish that's ideal for special occasions or a light, refreshing weeknight dinner, Skate Piccata is a delightful twist on the traditional Italian "piccata" preparation, usually made with veal or chicken. The mild, tender skate wing is seared and drenched in a bright, tangy lemon-caper sauce.

Why Piccata Skate?

The delicate flavor and distinct firm texture of skate complement the acidic and savory undertones of piccata sauce. Although skate isn't utilized as frequently as other fish like cod or halibut, it's a hidden seafood gem that elevates your menu. Made with butter, lemon, capers, and a little white wine, the piccata sauce adds a tangy richness that enhances the skate without dominating its delicate flavor.

Ingredients

4 skate wings, each weighing around 6 ounces

All-purpose flour (½ a cup) for dredging

To taste, add salt and pepper.

3 teaspoons of olive oil

1/4 cup of white wine

1/4 cup of freshly squeezed lemon juice (about two lemons)

2 teaspoons of drained capers

4 tablespoons of butter without salt

1/4 cup finely chopped fresh parsley

Slices of lemon (for garnish)

Instruction

In a saucepan, sauté the onion and garlic until they are soft and transparent. Then, add the white wine and soy and simmer for a few minutes. Finally, add the butter and whisk or swirl until it melts completely. Finally, add the lemon juice and salt and pepper. Simmer until the mixture is cohesive and well emulsified. Set aside.

Set up a typical breading station, flour, beaten egg, breadcrumbs all in separate bowls.

Place a big skillet over medium-high heat on the stove with olive oil.

Salt and pepper should be used to season the fish first, followed by flour (shake off excess flour), egg (till well coated), and breadcrumbs.

To ensure that the breadcrumbs adhere correctly, gently press the fish into them. Continue with the remaining fish.

When the oil in the hot pan shimmers and moves, the pan is ready for fish.

Carefully place the fish in the pan and give it a little shake to ensure that the oil coats the filet. Cook for 2 to 3 minutes, or until the desired color is achieved.

Use a spatula to flip. Continue with the remaining fish and let it rest on paper towels while the other filets cook.

Arrange the filets family-style on a big platter, cover with the desired quantity of sauce, and sprinkle with thyme and parsley.

Nutritional Benefits

Skate is a low-fat, lean protein source that is high in vitamins B12 and B6, which are critical for brain function and energy production. In addition to adding a delicious taste, the lemon juice and capers also contain antioxidants and vitamin C, which strengthens the immune system. This dish achieves a balance between richness and lightness by combining the healthful fats of butter and olive oil.

Serving:

Steamed veggies, sautéed spinach, or roasted asparagus are all excellent accompaniments to skate piccata. Serve it over rice pilaf, buttery mashed potatoes, or even just plain pasta with garlic and olive oil to mop up the rich sauce for a more substantial meal.

Conclusion: Skate Piccata is a fun and elegant way to eat seafood. It combines the strong tastes of lemon, butter, and capers with the distinctive texture of skate to create a dish that is simple to prepare and visually striking to display. A delightful seafood experience awaits you at Skate Piccata, whether you're preparing for a dinner party or treating yourself to a special lunch.

Roast Cajun Salmon with Black Beans and Avocado

This meal, Roast Cajun Salmon with Black Beans and Avocado, blends the richness of roasted salmon with the smoky, spicy flavor of Cajun seasoning. This dish, which is served with robust black beans and creamy avocado, is full of flavor and provides a good ratio of fiber, healthy fats, and proteins.

Why This Dish Works:

Salmon has a strong flavor that compliments strong flavors like Cajun spice and is naturally high in omega-3 fatty acids. The avocado adds a smooth, refreshing counterpoint to the Cajun seasoning's spice, while the black beans offer a filling, earthy element. This recipe combines a variety of flavors and textures, delighting the palette while being wholesome and simple to make.

Ingredients:

- 2 tablespoons of smoked paprika
- 1 teaspoon of dried oregano
- 1/2 a teaspoon of cayenne pepper (or a pinch if you like less heat)
- 1 tablespoon of light brown, soft sugar
- 2 zested limes, one juiced, and one wedged
- 1 smashed garlic clove
- 3 tablespoons of rapeseed or olive oil
- 3 peppers, chopped into pieces
- Peel and chop two red onions into wedges.
- 2 400g cans of black beans, drained, and an 850g salmon side that has been scaled and pin boned

Instruction

1. Heat the oven to 200°C or 180°C with a fan or gas. 6. In a bowl, combine the oil, lime zest, garlic, sugar, paprika, oregano, cayenne, and a generous amount of salt. In a large roasting tray, combine the peppers, onions, and beans with half of the spice paste. Bake for 25 minutes.

2. Take out of the oven and stir well with the beans and vegetables. Place the salmon skin-side down on top, and then drizzle the remaining spice paste over it. The salmon should be cooked through after another 25 minutes of baking.

3. In the meantime, cut the avocados and mango in half, stone them, and chop them finely for the salsa. Add the lime juice, salt, coriander, and chilli. Serve the beans, fish, and vegetables beside the salsa and wedges of lime for squeezing.

Nutritional Benefits.

There are a lot of nutrients in this cuisine. One of the greatest foods for heart-healthy omega-3 fatty acids, which lower inflammation and support cardiovascular health, is salmon. Selenium, vitamins D and B12, and high-quality protein are also abundant in it. Antioxidants, fiber, and plant-based protein found in black beans promote healthy digestion and help keep blood sugar levels stable. The avocado provides a creamy texture that counterbalances the spiciness of the Cajun salmon and adds beneficial monounsaturated fats, which are necessary for lowering cholesterol and improving brain function.

Differences:

Change the Protein: This recipe is also good with roasted chicken or shrimp if salmon isn't available or you prefer variation. Both do a fantastic job with the Cajun seasoning.

Vegetarian Option: Instead of using salmon, try using roasted sweet potatoes or tofu, combining them with the avocado and black beans and using the same Cajun seasoning.

Increase the Veggies: Serve this recipe with roasted bell peppers, sweet corn, or zucchini on the side for added nourishment.

With the ideal combination of flavors—spicy, smoky, creamy, and zesty—this Roast Cajun Salmon with Black Beans and Avocado recipe provides a nutritious, high-protein dinner that tastes decadent but is actually extremely nourishing. It's impressive enough to serve to guests, yet quick enough to prepare for a weeknight supper. This dish is as aesthetically pleasing as it is delicious thanks to the fresh avocado salsa, which also gives a lovely flash of color and freshness.

CHAPTER 12:

Poultry and Meat

Chicken and Vegetable Souvlaki

Vegetables with Chicken A tasty and colourful Mediterranean cuisine, souvlaki is ideal for a nutritious, satisfying dinner. This version of souvlaki, a classic Greek street snack, balances tender chicken with vibrant grilled veggies. Traditionally, souvlaki consists of marinated and skewered meat that is perfectly grilled.

Why Chicken and Vegetable Souvlaki?

The marinade, which is full of lemon, garlic, and herbs, gives the chicken a zesty, vibrant flavor that perfectly embodies Greek cooking. In addition to adding lovely color to the dish, the vegetables give the grilled chicken a sweet, smoky contrast. Chicken & Vegetable Souvlaki is a popular dish that provides a filling and healthy meal, whether it is prepared for a family dinner or a backyard BBQ.

Ingredients

4 skinless, boneless chicken breasts, sliced into small cubes
1 red bell pepper, chopped into small pieces
1 yellow bell pepper, chopped into small pieces
Slice one zucchini into rounds.

1 red onion, cut in quarters

1/4 cup of olive oil

2 lemons' juice

3 minced garlic cloves

2 teaspoons of oregano, dried

The dried thyme, one teaspoon

To taste, add salt and pepper.

Metal or wood skewers

Optional: Serving tzatziki sauce

Instruction

In a large, non-metallic basin, combine the oil, lemon juice, oregano, and garlic to make the marinade. Add the chicken. After covering, marinate for one hour in the refrigerator.

2 Alternatively, thread the onion, capsicums, and chicken onto skewers. Set a chargrill pan or barbeque to medium-high heat.

3. Until cooked through, grill the chicken and veggie skewers for 4–6 minutes (2–3 minutes per side).

Nutritional Benefits:

In addition to being incredibly tasty, chicken and vegetable souvlaki is also quite nutrient-dense. Lean and high-quality protein, chicken breast is vital for both muscle regeneration and general well-being. Bell peppers, zucchini, and onions are among the veggies that contribute a variety of vitamins (such as C and A), fiber, and antioxidants that promote heart health and your immune system. Healthy lipids, especially monounsaturated fats, which are excellent for heart health and inflammation management, are provided by the olive oil in the marinade.

Conclusion: Vegetables and Chicken The vivid tastes of the Mediterranean are brought to your table with the exquisitely simple yet delectable dish known as souvlaki. It's perfect as the centerpiece of your next picnic or as a quick and healthful weekday supper. With some lemon and Tzatziki on the side, it's difficult to resist the crowd-pleasing combination of charred veggies and delicious chicken! It is also highly adaptable, which makes it a dish that can be made to fit a wide range of palates.

Lemon Chicken Pasta with Spinach and Pine Nuts

Tender chicken, fresh spinach, and the crunch of toasted pine nuts are all combined in a zesty lemon sauce to create the vibrant, savory dish known as Lemon Chicken Pasta with Spinach and Pine Nuts. When you're craving something light but filling with a Mediterranean flair, this recipe is ideal.

This one-pan chicken pasta combines lean chicken breast and sautéed spinach for a one-bowl dish that's garlicky, lemony and best served with a little Parm on top. I named it "Mom's Skillet Pasta," and she called it "Devon's Favorite Pasta." In any case, it's a simple and quick weekday supper that we came up with together and wrote down on a small recipe card over ten years ago, and it's still a staple in my weekly dinner rotation. The whole family will enjoy this easy dinner.

Why **Lemon Chicken Pasta with Spinach and Pine Nuts?**

With the earthy greens and succulent chicken, the lemony sauce adds a delightfully refreshing tang. The rich, nutty flavor and lovely texture of toasted pine nuts enhance the other components. This recipe is a great choice for a special occasion or a quick weeknight dinner because it is both nutritious and tasty.

Ingredients

8 ounces of whole-wheat or gluten-free penne pasta

2 teaspoons of olive oil that is extra virgin

1 pound of skinless, boneless chicken breast or thighs that have been chopped into bite-sized pieces and, if needed, trimmed

1/2 a teaspoon of salt

1/2 a teaspoon of crushed pepper

4 minced garlic cloves

1/2 cup of white wine, dry

1 lemon's zest and juice

10 cups of freshly chopped spinach

4 tablespoons of Parmesan cheese, grated, separated

Instruction

Bring a big pot of water that has been salted to a boil. Pasta should be cooked as directed on the package until it is al dente. Save a cup of spaghetti water for later and drain and set aside.

Get the chicken ready:

Heat 1 tablespoon of olive oil in a large skillet over medium-high heat while the pasta cooks. Add the chicken pieces to the skillet after seasoning them with salt and pepper. Cook, flipping periodically, until the chicken is cooked through and golden brown, 6 to 8 minutes. Place the chicken on a platter and leave it there.

Add the spinach and garlic and sauté.

Add the remaining tablespoon of olive oil to the same skillet and reduce the heat to medium. Be cautious not to burn it when you add the minced garlic and sauté it for about a minute until it becomes aromatic.

Cook the chopped spinach for a further two to three minutes, stirring now and then, until it wilts.

Prepare the Lemon Sauce:

Add the red pepper flakes (if using), lemon juice, and lemon zest and stir. Give the mixture a minute to simmer. To make the sauce smooth, add a little of the pasta water you set aside if it appears too thick.

Mix and Serve:

Return the chicken and cooked pasta to the skillet along with the lemon sauce and spinach. Mix everything until it's evenly coated. Add the Parmesan cheese and toasted pine nuts, allowing the cheese to melt a little.

If necessary, add more salt and pepper to taste. Add extra pasta water until you get the consistency you want if you like a creamier texture.

Serve after garnishing:

Garnish with more Parmesan cheese and fresh parsley and serve hot. Before serving, squeeze some fresh lemon over the top to give the dish a little more brightness.

Nutritional Benefits:

In addition to being tasty, this lemon chicken pasta is nutrient-dense. Lean protein, which is necessary for muscle repair and general health, is found in chicken. Pine nuts provide protein, healthy fats, and essential vitamins including vitamin E, while spinach is high in iron, calcium, and antioxidants. Vitamin C is increased by the fresh lemon juice, and fiber can be added by using whole-grain pasta.

Simple ingredients are used to create a fresh, zesty, and filling dinner in Lemon Chicken Pasta with Spinach and Pine Nuts. It's ideal for anyone searching for a flavourful, quick, and healthful supper choice. This recipe is likely to please whether you're preparing it for your family, friends, or yourself.

Grilled Chicken Breasts with Lentils

A healthy, high-protein dish, Grilled Chicken Breasts with Lentils blends the earthy richness of lentils with the smokey, savory tastes of expertly grilled chicken. This dish, which provides a balanced combination of lean protein, fiber, and other nutrients, is not only very filling but also highly nutritious. Because it reheats well, it's perfect for a light dinner or meal prep.

Do you ever feel like you have too much information on food? I definitely do, but that doesn't stop me from consuming the work of the many excellent bloggers, chefs, and foodies that exist. Markets, eateries, blogs, social media posts, newspapers, and cookbooks are all great sources of inspiration. I've been following the recipe for Grilled Chicken Breasts with Lentil Salad for a while; it was created by two highly regarded culinary experts.

Why This Dish works

The chicken breasts retain their juicy meat while gaining a delightful charred taste from grilling. The lentils provide a substantial, nutrient-dense foundation that enhances the flavors of the chicken by absorbing the flavors of herbs and spices. This recipe is perfect for people who want to increase their intake of legumes because they are a fantastic plant-based source of protein.

Ingredients

10 Roma tomatoes, cut into six sections vertically

12 sprigs of thyme

3 tablespoons of olive oil

2 tablespoons of balsamic vinegar

Freshly ground black pepper and salt

1 medium red onion, cut thinly

3 tablespoons of premium red wine vinegar

4 tablespoons of olive oil

⅓ cup chopped Italian parsley leaves ½ cup chopped chives and three big minced garlic cloves

4 tablespoons. Exra Olive oil that is virgin

A package of 17½ ounces of Umbrian lentils

Four 2 to 2½-pound chicken breasts, skinless and boneless

Freshly ground black pepper and salt

To prepare the grill, use vegetable oil.

Drizzle with extra virgin olive oil

Instruction

1. Line a heavy-duty baking sheet with cooking parchment and preheat the oven to 250 degrees.
2. Spread the tomato segments so they don't crowd the baking sheet on the paper, cut side up. Drizzle the olive oil and balsamic vinegar over the tomatoes, scatter the thyme sprigs on top, and season with salt and freshly ground pepper.
3. After preheating the oven, place the tray inside and roast the tomatoes gently for two hours, or until they start to brown and shrivel. To ensure that

the tomatoes are roasted evenly, stir them twice throughout that time.

4. In a small bowl, marinate the thinly sliced red onion for 15 minutes with the red wine vinegar. In a basin big enough to hold the cooked lentils, combine the marinated onions, garlic, and 4 tablespoons olive oil.

5. Meanwhile, rinse the lentils with cold water in a colander. In a big heavy-duty pot, place the rinsed lentils and cover them with fresh, chilly water up to 1½ inches above the lentils. After bringing the lentils to a boil, lower the heat to a gentle simmer and cook, turning frequently, until they are cooked, 15 to 20 minutes. Because the little Umbrian lentils cook rapidly, check for doneness around 12 minutes in. Drain the lentils in a colander, making sure they are completely drained, and then add the warm cooked lentils to the bowl with the onion, garlic, and olive oil. You can do this a day ahead of time, let it cool, and then put it aside.

6. Transfer the chicken breast to a cutting board designated for chicken, which can be cleaned in the dishwasher. Using a meat pounder or small cast iron skillet, pound the meat until it is uniformly thickened, about ¾ to ½ inches thick. Repeat with the remaining chicken breasts, seasoning both sides with salt and freshly ground black pepper.

7. About 2 to 3 hours before serving, remove the lentil salad from the fridge and stir in all but 1 tablespoon of the parsley and chives. Cover with plastic wrap after arranging the lentil salad on a sizable serving plate.

8. Heat the grill until red hot and take the seasoned chicken breasts out of the fridge. At this stage, the grill ought to be completely free of any remaining debris. Apply a thin layer of vegetable oil to the grates using a

heat-resistant brush.

9. After the grill is ready, put the chicken breasts on it and cook for two to three minutes on each side. Before the two-minute mark, don't try to move the breast.

10. Transfer the chicken breasts straight to the lentil salad that has been plated. Sprinkle the remaining parsley and chives on top of the breasts after drizzling them with a little olive oil. The dish tastes great at room temperature but can be served right away.

Nutritional Benefits.

There are many health advantages to this food. Lean protein from chicken breasts aids in muscle regeneration and maintains feelings of fullness. Because of their high fiber, iron, and folate content, lentils can assist digestion and heart health. This dish is ideal for people who want to maintain a balanced diet because it is low in fat and high in vital nutrients due to the combination of chicken and lentils.

The main ingredients of this dish are straightforward, uncomplicated flavors that combine to produce a filling and healthy supper. Because it's so simple to make, grilled chicken breasts with lentils are a popular choice for hectic weeknights or menu planning. It's tasty, nutritious, and certain to become a kitchen mainstay.

Thyme Roast Chicken

A traditional and cozy recipe, Thyme Roast Chicken combines the earthy and fragrant flavor of fresh thyme with the warmth of roasted chicken. It's a straightforward yet sophisticated dish that works well for formal occasions as well as family gatherings. The goal of this recipe is to maximize taste with the least amount of work possible, allowing the chicken to be infused with thyme, garlic, and lemon as it roasts to perfection.

With its abundance of flavors, HelloFresh's Thyme Roast Chicken with Roast Veggies is the ideal choice for a supper night. Come up with a new beginning!

Facilities that handle peanuts, nuts, sesame, fish, crustaceans, milk, eggs, mustard, celery, soy, gluten, and sulphites pack the boxes and contents. Some products have had to use rapeseed oil instead of sunflower oil without changing the label because of the conflict in Ukraine. Rapeseed oil allergy reactions are uncommon, according to the FSA.

Why This Dish Works:

The high heat produces a gorgeous golden exterior that is crispy and tasty, while roasting the chicken with thyme and other fresh herbs brings out the inherent flavors of the meat. A sumptuous and filling dinner can be created by drizzling the chicken and any sides with the rich sauce made from the fluids released during roasting.

Ingredients

1 entire chicken (about 4-5 pounds)
2 tablespoons of dried thyme or a huge bunch of fresh thyme
1 lemon, cut in half
6 cloves of garlic, peeled and crushed
2 teaspoons of olive oil

To taste, add salt and pepper.

1 cup of water or chicken broth (optional for basting)

Fresh sprigs of thyme as a garnish

Instruction

1. Set the oven's temperature to 200°C. Cut the potatoes into wedges that are 2 cm wide; do not peel them. Place the wedges in a single layer on a large baking tray. Season with salt and pepper after drizzling with oil. Toss to coat, then lay out and bake for 30 to 35 minutes on the top level of your oven, or until golden. Halfway through cooking, turn. If need, use two baking trays; you want the potatoes to be evenly distributed.

2. Cut the red onion in half, peel it, and cut it into six wedges. Cut the carrot into quarters lengthwise and then cut into batons about 5 cm long (no need to peel). Slice the pepper into 1-cm-wide strips after halving it and removing the core. Chop the parsley roughly, including the stalks.

3. Place half of the dried thyme and a splash of oil in a bowl with the chicken. Add salt and pepper for seasoning. Add the seasoning to the chicken and massage it in. ESSENTIAL: After handling raw meat, wash your hands. Place the pepper, carrot, and red onion on a baking tray. Season with salt and pepper, drizzle with a little oil, then sprinkle with the remaining dried thyme. Toss to coat the vegetables, then bake for 25 to 30 minutes, or until they are tender and golden.

4. Heat a frying pan without oil over high heat. Add the chicken breasts and cook for 2 to 3 minutes on each side, or until browned. After it is browned, move it to your baking dish, place it on top of the vegetables, and continue to cook for another 15 to 20 minutes. Crucial: When the center of the chicken is no longer pink, it is done. You'll need your pan again in a minute, so don't wash it!

5. Add the water and chicken stock powder to the chicken frying pan (see ingredients for amount), bring to a boil, and then lower the heat to a simmer while the chicken roasts. After adding the chilli jam, bubble the liquid for three to four minutes until it thickens. Add salt and pepper for seasoning.

6. After cooking, take the wedges, chicken, and vegetables out of the oven. Cut each breast of chicken into five pieces. On one of the baking trays, combine the wedges, veggies, and chopped parsley; transfer to

plates using a spoon. If necessary, reheat the sweet chilli sauce before placing the chicken on top. Enjoy the chicken with the sweet chilli glaze spooned over it!

Nutritional Benefits:

This recipe is nutrient-dense in addition to being delicious. Lean and high-quality protein, chicken is vital for the immune system and muscle regeneration. With the addition of garlic's immune-boosting qualities and thyme's abundance of antioxidants, this roast is both tasty and healthy.

Serving:

Serve Thyme Roast Chicken with light arugula salad, roasted potatoes, or steamed green beans as easy sides. For a hearty, warming lunch, you may also serve it over buttered herb rice or a creamy mashed potato dish. The herbaceous undertones of the thyme are complemented by a crisp white wine such as Sauvignon Blanc or Chardonnay.

Conclusion: This recipe for Thyme Roast Chicken is classic, adaptable, simple to make, and consistently wonderful. This recipe is always a hit whether you're preparing it for a family get-together or simply want a filling, nutritious weeknight supper. Roasted chicken, lemon, garlic, and thyme combine to provide a delicious and enticing mixture that is difficult to refuse. Additionally, any leftovers are excellent for salads or sandwiches the next day!

Italian Baked Chicken Cacciatore

A substantial, rustic dish that is bursting with the deep aromas of Italian cooking is Italian Baked Chicken Cacciatore. Traditionally, "cacciatore"—which translates to "hunter" in Italian—is a hunter-style dinner prepared with readily available items from the countryside, such as chicken, tomatoes, mushrooms, herbs, and occasionally bell peppers or olives. It's a tasty and cosy meal that's ideal for entertaining guests with a home-cooked Italian dish or for a family evening.

A lonely can of stewed tomatoes in the cabinet served as the inspiration for this baked chicken cacciatore. This is very delicious and easy to make! This is delicious with rice or pasta, but I especially enjoy serving it with mashed potatoes. Feel free to "spice it up" whatever you like, but we prefer it just as is.

Why you'll love This Dish

The ideal combination of succulent, juicy chicken cooked in a flavourful tomato sauce enhanced with veggies, fresh herbs, and garlic is chicken cacciatore. While all the ingredients combine to create a flavourful, aromatic sauce, baking the dish guarantees that the chicken stays moist and soft. It's an easy one-pot supper that lets you experience Italian cuisine without putting in a lot of work.

Ingredients

4-6 skin-on, bone-in chicken thighs (or a combination of drumsticks and thighs)

2 teaspoons of olive oil

1 large onion, cut thinly

Thinly slice 2 bell peppers (choose orange, yellow, or red for sweetness).

3–4 minced garlic cloves

1 cup of sliced mushrooms (optional)

1 can (28 ounces) of crushed tomatoes

1/2 a cup of dry red wine or chicken broth (optional for further flavour depth)

2 teaspoons of oregano, dried

1 teaspoon of dried basil

1 bay leaf

To taste, add salt and pepper.

Chopped fresh parsley (for garnish)

For added freshness, fresh basil leaves are optional.

Grated Parmesan cheese (for serving, optional)

Instruction

Turn the oven on to 175 degrees Celsius (350 degrees Fahrenheit). Spray cooking spray on a 9 x 13-inch baking dish.

In a small basin, combine flour, garlic powder, 1/4 teaspoon salt, and pepper. Shake off any excess flour mixture after dredging the chicken in it.

In a large skillet, heat the oil over medium-high heat. Cook the chicken for 4 to 5 minutes on each side, or until it is beautifully browned. Place the chicken in the baking dish that has been prepared.

Add the garlic and onions to the skillet and cook for about five minutes, or until the onion is soft and transparent. Add the mushrooms and additional oil if needed, and cook for about five minutes, or until the mushrooms are tender. Add half a cup of wine to the pan, use a wooden spoon to scrape the browned food particles from the bottom, and heat for around five minutes, or until the liquid has evaporated. Add the remaining 1/4 teaspoon of salt, tomato sauce, and stewed tomatoes with juice. If the sauce seems too thick, add more wine and simmer for another minute or two. Cover the chicken in the baking dish with aluminium foil after pouring the mixture over it.

Bake for approximately 45 minutes in a preheated oven, or until the chicken is no longer pink at the bone and the juices flow clear. When placed close to the bone, an instant-read thermometer should register 165 degrees Fahrenheit (74 degrees Celsius).

Nutritional Benefits

In addition to being incredibly flavourful, this dish has a number of health advantages. High-quality protein is provided by the chicken thighs, and vitamins, antioxidants, and fibre are added by the tomatoes, peppers, and onions. Additionally, the dish contains heart-healthy lipids from the olive oil.

Conclusion: The classic recipe for Italian Baked Chicken Cacciatore embodies the essence of Italian home cooking in your kitchen. It's a soulful recipe that's ideal for entertaining friends or having a warm evening at home. This dish offers warmth and flavour with its aromatic tomato sauce, succulent chicken, and vibrant assortment of veggies. It will be a favourite with everyone who tastes it, whether you serve it with bread, pasta, or just a plain salad. Savour the simplicity and cosiness of Italian cooking with this mouthwatering chicken cacciatore!

Greek Pork Fillet with Mustard

Tender pork fillet and the strong, acidic flavour of mustard are expertly combined in this delectable and straightforward Mediterranean dish, Greek Pork Fillet with Mustard. For those seeking a tasty yet light main course, this dish, which is infused with traditional Greek ingredients like lemon, olive oil, and fresh herbs, is ideal. This recipe easily adds a touch of Greece to your table, whether you're preparing it for a special occasion or a weeknight supper.

Ingredients

1 pound (450 grams) of tenderloin, or pork fillet, with extra fat removed

3 teaspoons of olive oil

2 tablespoons of Dijon mustard (for texture, use whole grain mustard)

2 minced garlic cloves

1 lemon's juice

1 teaspoon of fresh or dried oregano, if available

To taste, add salt and pepper.

Garnish with fresh parsley or thyme, if desired.

Instruction

Set the oven's temperature to 160°C (320°F). arranged to fan

Score the pork diagonally, vertically, and skin-side.

Spread the lemon zest, finely sliced garlic, chili flakes, cloves, olive oil, salt, and pepper
over the entire surface of the pork loin after transferring it to a piece of parchment paper.

Line a baking sheet with a rack and cover with aluminium foil and parchment paper.

For three hours, roast. After 30 to 60 minutes, uncover and continue roasting.

Put the butter in a frying pan over medium heat.

Add the onion to the pan after coarsely chopping it.

Add the peppercorns, bay leaves, rosemary, thyme, and sauté.

Put one or two ladles of the sauce in a bowl, then whisk in the mustard until it dissolves.

Place the mustard sauce in the skillet and bring it to a boil for two to three minutes, or until it thickens.

Add the pickled cucumber to a bowl after finely chopping it. Set aside the sauce after draining it into the bowl containing the pickles.

After using the wine to deglaze the pan, add the chicken cube, water, and balsamic cream. Stir and bring to a boil for one to two minutes.

Nutritional Benefits

Because pork fillet is a lean, high-protein meat, it's a better option for people watching their fat intake. The mustard adds a little soreness without adding a lot of calories, and the olive oil offers heart-healthy fats. With the anti-inflammatory and antioxidant qualities of lemon and garlic, this dish is not only tasty but also nourishing.

Serving

Serve this Greek pork fillet with mustard with traditional sides like quinoa salad, steamed vegetables, or roasted potatoes.

A Greek Assyrtiko or a crisp white wine like Sauvignon Blanc will go well with the tastes of mustard and lemon.

Serve it with pita bread, grilled veggies, and tzatziki for a Mediterranean-style feast.

Conclusion:

This Greek Pork Fillet with Mustard is a fantastic illustration of how a few basic components can come together to make a tasty and visually striking dish. Anyone who enjoys Mediterranean flavours will appreciate this recipe since it has the depth of garlic and oregano, the brightness of lemon, and the tang of mustard. It's a filling, healthful dish that's simple to make and sophisticated enough to serve at a gathering. Savor this dish with.

Estouffade d'Agneau

The traditional French lamb stew, estouffade d'Agneau, is slow-cooked to perfection, producing tasty, delicate meat that is enhanced by earthy, rich vegetables and fragrant herbs. This classic Provençal dish, which uses straightforward, healthful ingredients to provide a filling and substantial supper, epitomises rustic French cuisine.

Ingredients

2 pounds (900 grams) of large-cut lamb shoulder

2 teaspoons of olive oil

1 big onion, diced

3 minced garlic cloves

2 carrots, sliced and peeled

2 chopped celery stalks

1 cup (240 millilitres) of dry red wine, such as a Côtes du Rhône wine

1 cup (240 ml) of lamb or beef stock

1 spoonful of tomato paste

1 bay leaf

A couple of fresh rosemary and thyme sprigs (or one teaspoon of) To taste, add salt and pepper.

Instruction

Cook the Vegetables: In the same pot, add the chopped onion, carrots, and celery. Sauté for about five minutes, until the vegetables start to soften and the onions turn golden. Add the minced garlic and cook for an additional minute until fragrant. Sear the Lamb: Heat the olive oil in a large, heavy-bottomed pot or Dutch oven over medium-high heat. Season the lamb chunks with salt and pepper, then brown them in batches, making sure they are seared on all sides. This step improves flavour.

Deglaze with Wine:

- Pour the red wine into the pot, using a wooden spoon to scrape up any browned bits from the bottom of the pot. This step, known as deglazing, brings out deep flavors.
- Let the wine simmer for about 3-5 minutes to reduce slightly and cook off the alcohol.

Add the Lamb and Broth:

- Return the browned lamb to the pot, along with the tomato paste, bay leaf, thyme, and rosemary.
- Pour in the beef or lamb stock, ensuring the liquid just covers the lamb and vegetables. Bring everything to a simmer.

Slow Cook:

- Cover the pot and reduce the heat to low. Let the stew cook gently for 1.5 to 2 hours, stirring occasionally, until the lamb is very tender and the flavours have melded together beautifully.
- If the stew becomes too dry during cooking, you can add a little more stock or water.

A little additional stock or water can be added if the stew gets too dry while cooking.

Serve:

Remove the herb sprigs and bay leaf from the lamb after it is tender.

If necessary, add extra salt and pepper to adjust the seasoning.

Serve the Estouffade d'Agneau hot, with buttered noodles, creamy mashed potatoes, or rustic bread to mop up the flavourful sauce. If you'd like, garnish with fresh herbs.

Nutritional Benefit

Packed with vital vitamins and minerals including iron, zinc, and vitamin B12, lamb is a wonderful source of high-quality protein. This nutritious recipe gains fibre and antioxidants from the addition of veggies like celery and carrots. Cooking with fresh herbs and olive oil adds nutrition and heart-healthy fats.

In conclusion, estouffade d'Agneau is a classic, hearty dish that embodies the cosiness and warmth of French cooking. This recipe promises to give rich, deep tastes with little effort, whether you're cooking it for a family feast or savouring it on a chilly evening. Simple items are transformed into a filling and unforgettable meal through the slow-cooking method. Savour this filling lamb stew with your preferred sides for a very rustic French meal.

Involtini di Manzo

Involtini di Manzo is a delectable Italian dish composed of thin slices of beef folded up and stuffed with flavourful ingredients like cheese, herbs, and sometimes vegetables. The rolls are then cooked in a rich tomato sauce until tender and juicy, creating a dish that's both comfortable and elegant.

The combination of tender beef, a savoury stuffing, and the depth of flavour from the slow-simmered tomato sauce makes this dish irresistible. It's also versatile, as you can alter the stuffing to your preference, making it a great go-to recipe for any occasion. This dish is the pinnacle of Italian comfort food, yet sophisticated enough to impress at a dinner party.

ROLL ALEX

Ingredients

1/2 cups of olive oil,

2 tablespoons of unsalted butter,

2 cups of finely chopped peeled carrots,

1 cup of finely chopped onion,

2 cloves of minced garlic,

1/2 cups of grated parmesan cheese, salt and freshly ground black pepper, to taste, eight beef scallopini (long and very thin, Milanese cut), all-purpose flour for dredging, 1/2 cups of dry white wine,

1 bay leaf, one can of diced tomatoes in tomato puree,

1 and a half cups of frozen peas,

2 cups of frozen peas,

2 ounces of coarsely chopped prosciutto

Instruction

1. In 1 tablespoon of oil and 1 tablespoon of butter, sauté the carrots, onion, and garlic until the carrots are soft. After adding salt and pepper, turn off the heat. Add the parmesan after letting it cool a little.

2. Use salt and pepper to season the beef. Put two tablespoons of carrot mix in the center of each beef slice's wider end. To wrap the filling, roll up the slices from the

wide end, tucking the sides in. Use toothpicks or poultry laces to secure the end.

3. Heat the butter and remaining oil over medium-high heat. The meat rolls should be lightly dredged in flour. Brown on all sides after adding to the pan. Scrape up the browned bits from the bottom and add the wine. Add the bay leaf and the tomatoes, stirring gently. For five to ten minutes, or until the steak is cooked through, cover and simmer. Place the beef buns on a platter and leave them to rest.

4. Stir the prosciutto and peas into the pan's sauce, then boil until the sauce has slightly reduced and the peas are well heated. Adjust the seasoning to your preference.

5. After removing the picks from the beef rolls, cover the rolls with the sauce.

Serving

Pasta: Pasta is frequently served with involtini di manzo. The ideal accompaniment is a simple dish of rigatoni or spaghetti tossed with butter or olive oil.

Serve the beef rolls over a creamy polenta for a more rustic look. The polenta will absorb the rich tomato sauce well.

Grilled Vegetables: A side of roasted peppers, eggplant, or zucchini brings colour and harmony to the dish.

Conclusion: Involtini di Manzo is a dish that exemplifies the elegance of Italian cooking: basic ingredients combine to produce a genuinely unique dish. This meal adds heart and warmth to the table whether it's being prepared for a regular supper or served at a special event.

Algerian Mderbe

A traditional dish with roots in Algeria's rich culinary heritage is Algerian Mderbe. This filling dish features lamb and green beans in a tasty tomato-based sauce that is seasoned with fragrant North African spices including cinnamon, paprika, and cumin. This hearty, slow-cooked dish is ideal for bringing loved ones together around the table.

Why Is Algerian Mderbe Unique?

The robust flavours of Mderbe, which are savoury, somewhat spicy, and incredibly fulfilling, are characteristic of Algerian cuisine. The earthy green beans and tender lamb cooking in a fragrant sauce exemplify how spices may be used to enhance basic foods. It's a traditional example of a North African stew, which is prepared slowly to allow the flavours to combine and produce a dish that is full of depth and warmth.

Ingredients

500g of cubed lamb (shoulder or leg)

300g of clipped green beans

1 onion, chopped finely

2 to three minced garlic cloves

1 cup of tomato purée or two tomatoes, diced and skinned

1 spoonful of tomato paste

1 teaspoon of cumin powder

1 teaspoon of paprika

1/2 a teaspoon of cinnamon powder

To taste, add salt and pepper.

Olive oil

Chopped fresh parsley or coriander (for garnish)

Vegetable broth or water

Instruction

To prepare the lamb, heat a big heavy-bottomed saucepan over medium heat with a couple teaspoons of olive oil. Season with salt and pepper as you go, then add the cubed lamb and brown it on all sides. When the lamb is browned, take it out of the pot and put it aside.

Sauté the Vegetables: In the same saucepan, cook the chopped onion until it is tender and transparent, adding a little extra olive oil if needed. Cook for an additional minute after adding the minced garlic, taking care not to let it burn.

Enhance the Taste: Allow the spices to bloom in the pan's heat for approximately one minute after adding the cumin, paprika, and ground cinnamon. Their fragrant oils will be released, enhancing the dish's flavour.

Stir everything together after adding the chopped tomatoes (or tomato purée) and tomato paste. For a rich tomato base, boil this for 5 to 10 minutes.

Bring the stew to a simmer: Add enough water or broth to cover the browned lamb when it has been returned to the pot. After bringing the mixture to a boil, lower the heat and put a lid on the pot. Allow the stew to simmer slowly for approximately an hour, or until the lamb is cooked.

Include the green beans: Stir the green beans into the lamb after it has been cooking for around one hour. Simmer the stew for a further 20 to 30 minutes, or until the beans are soft but still have some firmness. You can add a bit of extra water or broth if the sauce gets too thick.

Serve after garnishing:

Taste the stew and adjust the seasoning if necessary once the lamb and green beans are cooked through. For a splash of colour and freshness, garnish with freshly chopped parsley or coriander.

To absorb the rich sauce, serve the Mderbe hot with rice, crusty bread, or couscous.

Nutritional Benefits

In addition to being a fantastic source of high-quality protein, lamb also contains important vitamins and minerals like iron, zinc, and vitamin B12.

Green beans give a nutritious vegetable element that balances the richness of the lamb while also contributing fibre, vitamins, and antioxidants to the meal.

This recipe is not only tasty but also health-conscious because of the addition of tomatoes and spices, which provide healthy antioxidants like lycopene and anti-inflammatory qualities.

Serving.

A classic accompaniment to Mderbe is a fluffy couscous, which gives the rich stew a light, airy foundation.

Crusty Bread: To mop up the flavourful sauce, a piece of crusty bread is ideal.

Simple Salad: To balance the dish, serve it with a crisp salad dressed with lemon and olive oil.

Conclusion: Algerian Mderbe is a celebration of the robust, robust flavours of Algerian cuisine rather than merely a meal. For a family meal, a get-together with friends, or any other occasion where you want to serve something hearty but unique, this lamb and green bean stew is ideal. Mderbe is a delectable way to sample the rich flavours of North African food, regardless of your familiarity with it.

Pork Pot Roast with Apples

A remarkable recipe for any occasion, pork pot roast with apples strikes the ideal balance between savoury and sweet flavours. The natural sweetness of apples, accentuated with flavourful herbs and spices, is a perfect match for the succulent, slow-cooked pork. This recipe is perfect for holiday get-togethers, warm family dinners, or any time you want a sophisticated yet comforting supper.

Apple sauce goes well with roast pork. Simply chop, peel, and core some apples. Add them to a pot along with orange zest, brown sugar, and butter. Make apple sauce by cooking them until they crumble.

If you dislike apple sauce, you'll always find mustard. I'm not referring to mustard for yellow hot dogs. That is for children. A good, hearty mustard is what you need. A blend of spicy brown and whole grain varieties might work well. Pickles, too. Pickles are a must if you have mustard and meat.

Mostarda di Frutta would be my final recommendation. With the Italian condiment mostarda, you can have the best of both worlds. Mostarda is produced by stewing fruits in a sweet and sour syrup with a dash of mustard seed, much like a chutney. Any mix of fruits, including apples, peaches, cherries, figs, pears, and grapes, can be used to make it. It goes really well with roasted pork.

Ingredients

1 roast of pork loin or shoulder (4-5 lbs)

4 to five apples, peeled and sliced (ideally a combination of sweet and tart types, such as Granny Smith and Honeycrisp)

4 to five minced garlic cloves and two big onions, sliced

2 cups of vegetable or chicken broth

1 cup of apple juice or cider

2 to three fresh rosemary sprigs (or one teaspoon of dried rosemary)

2 to three fresh thyme sprigs (or one teaspoon of dried thyme)

2 tablespoons of olive oil

To taste, add salt and pepper.

2 tablespoons of Dijon mustard (optional, for added flavour depth)

For a thicker sauce, you can add one or two tablespoons of butter.

Instruction

Season the pork.

Season the pork roast well on all sides with salt and pepper. Apply Dijon mustard to the pork to enhance its flavour.

Sear the pork.

In a heavy-bottomed pot or large Dutch oven, heat the olive oil over medium-high heat. Sear the pork roast until it is beautifully browned on all sides. In addition to adding a lovely caramelised coating of flavour, this step seals in the fluids. After the pork has seared, take it out of the pot and put it aside.

Add the garlic and onions and sauté.

If needed, add a little extra olive oil to the same saucepan and cook the onions until they are tender and beginning to turn brown. Cook for an additional minute after adding the minced garlic, stirring often to prevent burning.

Build the Sauce and Deglaze:

After adding the chicken stock and apple cider (or apple juice), scrape out any browned bits from the bottom of the kettle. These "fond," or browned bits, are incredibly flavourful. Bring the liquid to a gentle simmer.

Include the herbs and apples:

Arrange the fresh herbs (thyme and rosemary) and sliced apples in layers around the pot. You can now add a little more apple cider if you prefer a slightly sweeter sauce.

Put the Pork Back in the Pot:

Place the apple and onion combination on top of the seared pork and nestle it back into the pot. To keep the pork wet while it slow-cooks, it should be partially immersed in the liquid.

Slow Cooking:

Put a tight-fitting lid on the saucepan and turn the heat down to low. For two to three hours, or until the pork is soft and can be easily torn apart with a fork, let it cook slowly. Another option is to move the pot to an oven set to 325°F (160°C) and bake it for the same length of time.

Complete the Sauce:

After the pork is cooked, take it out of the pot and give it time to rest. Add 1-2 tablespoons of butter to the apple mixture and stir to create a thicker sauce. To make the sauce a little thicker, simmer it for a few minutes.

Serve:

Serve the pork with the apples and onions, sliced or shred, and drizzled with the sauce. Add more fresh herbs as a garnish if desired

Nutritional Benefits.

Iron, protein, and several important B vitamins—particularly niacin and vitamin B12—are all found in pork. These nutrients boost metabolism and help sustain energy levels.

Vitamins, antioxidants, and fibre are all found in apples. Additionally, they naturally sweeten food without the need for added sugar, giving it a delicious yet light texture.

Garlic and onions add taste and health advantages to the dish because of their well-known heart-healthy and anti-inflammatory qualities.

Serving.

Mashed Potatoes: A traditional accompaniment to pork pot roast are creamy mashed potatoes, which absorb the flavourful apple-onion sauce.

Roasted Vegetables: Roasted parsnips, Brussels sprouts, or carrots give the dish a deliciously caramelised taste.

Crusty Bread: A delicious loaf of crusty bread completes the supper and is ideal for soaking up the tasty sauce.

Conclusion

Pork Pot Roast with Apples is a delicious recipe that has a sophisticated yet rustic vibe. It's simple to make and elegant enough to serve at a formal dinner party. This meal is a huge hit because of the mix of sweet apples and delicate pork cooking in a flavourful broth. This hearty dish will please everyone, whether you're preparing it for family or visitors.

CHAPTER 13:

Eggs

One of the most nutrient-dense and adaptable foods is eggs. They are essential to many different cuisines and recipes around the world, whether they are scrambled, poached, boiled, or baked. A staple in many diets, eggs are well-known for their high protein content and provide a distinctive mix of flavour and texture in addition to a number of health advantages.

Eggs, long condemned by heart disease specialists and well-meaning doctors for their high cholesterol content, appear to be making a slight resurgence. What then changed? Eggs have other nutrients that may help reduce the risk of heart disease, even though one big egg yolk contains 200 mg of cholesterol, making it one of the greatest sources of dietary cholesterol. Furthermore, the majority of an egg's mild 5 grams of fat are monounsaturated and polyunsaturated fat. (Source: food-features/eggs/ on https://nutritionsource.hsph.harvard.edu)

Why Are Eggs Such a Nutritious Food?

Eggs are a great source of vital nutrients. About 6 grams of high-quality protein, which includes all nine essential amino acids, can be found in one big egg. Eggs are also a great source of the following vitamins and minerals:

Red blood cell formation and brain health depend on vitamin B12.

Vitamin D: Promotes immunological and bone health.

Choline: Vital for the liver and brain, and crucial during pregnancy.

One potent antioxidant that helps shield cells from harm is selenium.

The Components of an egg

Whites of eggs: The egg whites are minimal in calories and fat and primarily composed of protein and water. They are perfect for people who want to eat more protein without gaining excess weight.

The majority of the egg's contents, such as vitamins, minerals, and good fats, are found in the yolks. Although evidence indicates that dietary cholesterol from eggs does not significantly affect blood cholesterol levels for the majority of people, the yolk does contain cholesterol.

Using Eggs in Cooking: Eggs are a versatile ingredient that can be used in anything from gourmet recipes to quick breakfasts. Here are some traditional and inventive egg cooking methods

Scrambled: Ideal for breakfast, it's fluffy and soft. They can be as basic as you like or as elaborate as you desire (with cheese, vegetables, and herbs, for example).

Poached: A little more delicate, poached eggs work well in salads or in recipes like eggs Benedict.

Hard-Boiled: These make a handy addition to sandwiches, salads, or snacks. Additionally, they keep well in the refrigerator for a few days.

Omelets: A filling breakfast option at any time of day, omelets can be loaded with cheeses, meats, or veggies.

Baked: Eggs become delectable savoury dishes that can be eaten for breakfast, lunch, or dinner when baked into quiches, frittatas, or casseroles.

Eggs in Baking

Because of their structural qualities, eggs are necessary in baking. They provide cakes, biscuits, and pastries with their richness, wetness, and binding power. While yolks provide smooth custards that give a variety of dishes depth and texture, egg whites can be whipped into meringues.

Are Eggs Nutritious?

The cholesterol content of eggs has been a topic of discussion, but recent studies have demonstrated that, for the majority of people, eggs may be included in a heart-healthy diet without significantly raising blood cholesterol levels. They are satisfying due to their high protein content, which can aid with appetite control and weight management.

Types of Egg

The most popular kind of eggs are chicken eggs, which come in a range of sizes and hues from white to brown. Every colour has the same nutritional value.

Duck eggs are used frequently in gourmet cookery because they are larger than chicken eggs and have a deeper flavour.

Quail Eggs: Often used in appetisers or as a garnish, quail eggs are little but incredibly flavourful.

The labels "free-range" and "organic" eggs describe the hens' raising practices. Organic eggs are produced by hens that are fed organic feed, whereas free-range hens have access to the outdoors.

Why you Need Eggs in Your Diet

Eggs are nutrient-dense, inexpensive, and easily available. You can support muscle growth and maintenance, give you sustained energy, and improve the health of your heart and brain by including them in your diet. With their many culinary applications, eggs provide many advantages, whether you're trying to eat healthier or are just searching for a simple protein that's quick to prepare.

Conclusion

Eggs are a real kitchen essential that provide convenience and nutrition. Eggs can be used for any meal or occasion, from straightforward scrambled eggs to more complex creations like frittatas or soufflés. They can readily be included in a balanced and healthful diet due to their extensive list of vitamins, minerals, and health advantages.

CHAPTER 14:

Breads, Flatbreads, Pizzas, and More

With "Breads, Flatbreads, Pizzas, and More," you're exploring the essence of international cooking. From rustic loaves to thin, crispy flatbreads and all in between, these mainstays have been at the heart of culinary traditions for ages. These products provide comfort, taste, and adaptability to the table whether you're baking bread from home or throwing together a quick pizza for supper.

Breads: An International Mainstay

One of the first prepared foods is bread, which is made and consumed almost everywhere in the world. From fluffy and light to hearty and dense, it can take many different forms. Bread's simplicity—flour, water, yeast, and salt—is what makes it so beautiful, but with the right ingredients and methods, it can be made into something truly remarkable.

Artisan bread is baked using a slow fermentation process, usually resulting in a firm crust and a light, airy middle. Ciabatta, sourdough loaves, and French baguettes are a few examples.

Made with whole wheat or other grains like rye, barley, or oats, whole grain bread has a higher fibre content and a thicker texture, making it ideal for people who are health-conscious.

Baking soda or powder is used to leaven quick breads instead of yeast. They include items like zucchini bread, cornbread, and banana bread and are quick to prepare.

Flatbreads: The Versatile Base

Simple breads known as "flatbreads" are produced with little or no rising agent or without yeast (unleavened). They are thin and adaptable, and in many cultures they are used as wraps, snacks, or as a foundation for toppings.

Pita: A Middle Eastern flatbread that is soft and somewhat leavened, it is frequently split open to accommodate salads, shawarma, or falafel.

Naan: An Indian flatbread that is soft and pillowy and is usually prepared in a tandoor oven. Naan is ideal as a basis for toppings or as a dip for curries.

A mainstay of Mexican cooking, tortillas are prepared from either corn or wheat and are used in tacos, quesadillas, and burritos, among other foods.

Lavash: An Armenian thin, unleavened flatbread that's perfect for encasing meats, veggies, or dips.

A typical Indian flatbread made with whole wheat flour, roti or chapati is frequently eaten with stews and curries.

Pizza: A Global Favourite

Despite its Italian roots, pizza has gained popularity all over the world and has undergone numerous modifications that are influenced by regional ingredients and tastes.

Classic Neapolitan Pizza: This is the pizza that got it all began, including a soft, chewy crust, fresh mozzarella, basil, and San Marzano tomatoes.

Pizza with a thin, crunchy crust is ideal if you want to draw attention to the toppings rather than the bread.

A thick, spongy pizza that is baked in a square or rectangle shape and frequently topped with cheese, herbs, and tomato sauce is known as Sicilian pizza.

Chicago Deep Dish Style: With its layers of cheese, meats, and sauce, this thick, pie-like pizza is more of a substantial dinner than a snack.

Chicago-Style Deep Dish: More of a substantial meal than a snack, this pizza is deep and pie-like, with layers of cheese, meats, and sauce.

Often made using naan, pita, or handmade dough, flatbread pizza is a lighter and faster option to traditional pizza. It can be topped with anything from traditional tomato sauce to cutting-edge toppings like goat cheese, arugula, or prosciutto.

The Role of Bread in the Meal

Bread's Function in Meals Bread is frequently seen as the focal point or side dish of many meals. The meal can begin with a straightforward bread basket filled with slices, rolls, or breadsticks and served with olive oil or butter. As with paninis, open-faced toasts, and sandwiches, it can also be the main attraction.

You may customise pizzas and flatbreads in countless ways while still enjoying the ease of a quick lunch. From a traditional Margherita pizza to a gourmet flatbread topped with figs, blue cheese, and honey, you can make it as simple or as complex as you wish.

Homemade vs. Store-Bought

It can be immensely fulfilling to bake bread at home. From the type of flour to any additional seasonings, the procedure gives you complete control over the ingredients. However, if you select premium, artisanal breads, store-bought breads can taste just as good.

Pizza dough and flatbreads are similarly simple to create at home, but store-bought varieties offer a quick and practical foundation for homemade dishes. The allure of pizzas and flatbreads is that they can be used as a blank canvas for a wide range of ingredients and flavours.

Concluding remarks

"Breads, Flatbreads, Pizzas, and More" combines the best of comfort cuisine from throughout the world. These meals offer something for every taste and occasion, whether you're enjoying a newly baked sourdough loaf, the crisp bite of a well-made flatbread, or a slice of pizza topped with your favourite ingredients. They symbolise the kind of healthy, fulfilling food that unites people and make the ideal base for meals, snacks, or sides.

A delightful blend of sweet, acidic, and creamy flavours, "Labneh with Honeyed Figs" feels decadent yet light and crisp. Similar to cream cheese, labneh is a thick, velvety Middle Eastern strained yoghourt that has a cool, tangy flavour. It's the ideal foundation for combining with a wide range of ingredients, and it becomes a sophisticated yet straightforward dish when honeyed figs are added on top.

One of the most popular dishes in the Middle East is labneh. I grew up eating it and really like it because I'm half Armenian. On the weekends, my great-grandmother and grandmother would prepare a new batch to consume. The greatest is always fresh. Actually, a lot of Mediterranean eateries provide labneh. beneath the menu's mezzo section. It can be served as a dip with sumac, olive oil, and a variety of other ingredients. However, it's also very easy to create at home. Waiting a whole day for it to become somewhat thicker is the most difficult aspect.

Labneh is a soft cheese if you haven't heard of it before. To make that, the yoghurt is strained to get rid of the extra liquid and whey. The texture will resemble cream cheese quite a bit as a result. Because it's prepared with yoghurt, it has a beautifully creamy flavour with a faint tang.

What Is Unique About Labneh?

In essence, labneh is yoghourt that has been strained to get rid of extra liquid, giving it a thick, creamy texture. Though it resembles Greek yoghourt, labneh is thicker and frequently used as a dip or spread. It is a versatile base for both savoury and sweet meals because of the subtle tang from the yoghourt cultures, which provides a refreshing contrast to richer, more decadent toppings.

Honeyed Figs: A Natural Sweetness

When figs are ripe and full of flavor, they provide a distinct sweetness to this dish. They complement the creamy labneh well because of their jammy texture and delicate, organic honey-like flavor. Incorporating a small amount of real honey into the figs brings out their inherent sweetness and creates a nice contrast with the tart yogurt. The honey gives the figs a glossy finish and enhances their flavor, resulting in a bite that is rich but well-balanced.

Put a Final Touch

You can top with chopped walnuts or pistachios to give even more layers of flavour. The soft and creamy textures are delightfully contrasted with the crunch of the almonds. The dish will also become more complicated with a sprinkle of sea salt, a pinch of za'atar spice, or a drizzle of olive oil (particularly if you're going for a more savoury version).

A Versatile Dish

The adaptability of Labneh with Honeyed Figs is among its best features. Because it falls somewhere between savoury and sweet, it can be used for any occasion or time of day. Whether you want a simple yet filling dessert, a quick and healthy breakfast, or a visually appealing appetisers for this dish's flavour, texture, and visual appeal make it an excellent choice for entertaining.,

Ingredients

1 cup of Greek yoghourt with full fat

1/4 teaspoon sea salt

1.5 tablespoons of raw honey

3 quartered figs

1/2 a lemon, zested

Chopped walnuts, 2 tablespoons

1 tablespoon of freshly chopped basil

Optional: a little pinch of sumac

Instruction

Combine the yogurt and sea salt in a bowl.

Depending on how thick your yogurt is, you may need to scoop the mixture onto two layers of cheesecloth.

To ensure that the labneh hangs in the middle of a medium bowl without touching the bottom, bring the sides of the cheesecloth together, knot it around a wooden spoon, and position the spoon across the top of the bowl. Overnight, chill.

Place the labneh on a dish after removing it from the cheesecloth. Drizzle with honey after adding the figs, walnuts, lemon zest, and basil.

Enjoy it with bread, crackers, or fresh cucumbers.

In summary, "Labneh with Honeyed Figs" is a celebration of balance: the honey brings out the natural sugars in the fruit, while the creamy, tangy labneh balances the sweet, syrupy figs. This dish combines sophistication and simplicity, making it a great option for any occasion where you want to impress without a lot of fuss.

Baked Peaches with Greek Yogurt and Almonds

In a single, easy meal, "Baked Peaches with Greek Yogurt and Almonds" embodies the perfect balance of comfort and nourishment. This recipe, which combines the natural sweetness of ripe peaches with the creamy tang of Greek yogurt and a satisfying crunch from toasted almonds, is ideal as a light dessert, breakfast treat, or snack. When combined, these components produce a flavourful and well-balanced experience.

Why Peaches Baked?

Peaches' natural sugars are enhanced and their flesh is softened by baking, giving them a warm, jammy consistency that is decadent but still surprisingly light. The tanginess of the yoghourt and the nutty flavours of the almonds are complemented by the caramelised sweetness that the heat brings out in the peaches.

The Role of Greek Yoghourt

The juicy peaches are balanced by the creamy texture of Greek yogurt. Because of its inherent thickness, it pairs well with baked fruits because it doesn't get watery when layered on top. This dish's high protein level also makes it filling and stimulating, while the yogurt's subtle tang balances the peaches' sweetness.

Almonds for a Nutty Crunch

In addition to adding a wonderful crunch, toasted almonds add a subtle nuttiness that accentuates the flavours in this dish. Because almonds are high in protein and good fats, this treat is as nourishing as it is tasty. You may either mix chopped almonds with a little cinnamon or sprinkle them straight on top of the yogurt.

Ingredients

Play around with what's in season and use
  1 ripe peach (you can also use a pear or apple)
  2 tsp olive oil,

2 tsp maple syrup,

flaky sea salt,

1/3 cup Greek yogurt,

1/4 cup your preferred granola,

a drizzle of honey and cinnamon on top.

Instruction

Set the oven's temperature to 350 degrees.

Halve your peach and scoop out the pit. Transfer to a baking dish and pour maple syrup and olive oil over it. To ensure that the peach is coated uniformly, use a brush. Bake for 25 to 30 minutes after adding a pinch of flakey sea salt.

Add granola, Greek yogurt, honey, and cinnamon on top.

Concluding remarks

A wonderful celebration of whole ingredients, "Baked Peaches with Greek Yogurt and Almonds" allows each item to shine. This recipe offers rich, nuanced flavours and textures while embodying simplicity. This combination will provide cosiness and contentment to any table, whether it is served as a nutritious breakfast, a healthy dessert, or a cosy snack.

Buttermilk Panna Cotta with Raspberries

A contemporary take on a traditional Italian dessert, buttermilk panna cotta with raspberries has a smooth, creamy texture and a touch of acidity that wonderfully counterbalances its sweetness. A sophisticated option for a dinner party finale, a special breakfast treat, or a weekend indulgence, this panna cotta is light but decadent.

This is pannacotta made with buttermilk. Gelatine thickens milk pudding and buttermilk, giving it a tangy, light consistency similar to yogurt.

I could easily eat this every day, topped with fresh raspberries and strawberries, and the best part is that I wouldn't feel bad about it because it only has 126 calories!

On the surface, the panna cotta looks like a rich, creamy creme brulee or flan.

However, one spoonful contradicts this: "So light! So cool! And so fulfilling!" Yes, friends, this is panna cotta, the lesser-known but excellent cousin of custard.

The Perfect Balance of Flavors

The distinct flavour characteristic of buttermilk panna cotta is what sets it apart. Buttermilk elevates the panna cotta's smoothness without adding weight by providing a hint of acidity. This kind of panna cotta tastes fresher than classic panna cotta, which makes it a great choice to combine with fresh fruit like raspberries. Bright, gratifying, and refreshingly light, the balance of flavours is created by the tartness of the raspberries and the creamy buttermilk.

The Role of Raspberries

Buttermilk panna cotta is the ideal partner for raspberries.

Their inherent acidity transforms the panna cotta from plain to spectacular by slicing through the smoothness and adding a splash of vivid colour. The luscious, slightly acidic flavour of fresh raspberries makes for a lovely contrast that is both elegant and revitalising. For a layered appearance and flavour, you can use whole berries and sauce, drizzle a light raspberry coulis over them, or distribute them over the panna cotta.

Ingredients

2 tablespoons of water

1½ tablespoons of gelatin without flavor

Coconut oil for ramekin lubrication

1 cup of whole milk

1/2 a cup of sugar

1 teaspoon of lemon peel, finely grated

1 rosemary sprig

2 cups of buttermilk

Berries as a garnish

Instruction

In a small bowl, combine the gelatin and water. Give it fifteen minutes or so to soften the gelatin. Six ¾-cup ramekins should be lightly sprayed with nonstick spray.

1. In a medium saucepan, heat the milk, sugar, lemon peel, and rosemary over medium-high heat. Stir continuously until the sugar melts.

2. Raise the heat and, with occasional stirring, bring to a gentle boil. After adding the gelatin mixture, turn off the heat. Until the gelatin dissolves, stir. Stir frequently while you cool the mixture to lukewarm. Divide the mixture among the prepared ramekins after

stirring in the buttermilk. Put panna cotta in the fridge for about 4 hours or until it sets.

3. Cut around the panna cotta in each ramekin with a small, sharp knife. To enable the panna cotta to settle onto the platter, place a plate over each ramekin and invert. Serve cold with berries on top.

Concluding remarks

The dessert Buttermilk Panna Cotta with Raspberries is as visually appealing as it is delicious, with each ingredient expertly blended to provide a rich and revitalizing experience. This panna cotta is ideal for entertaining without spending a lot of time in the kitchen because of its simple preparation and sophisticated presentation. Comfort, style, and the freshness of seasonal berries are all combined in this dessert, which is perfect for entertaining or indulging yourself.

THE MEDITERRANEAN DIET COOKBOOK FOR BEGINNERS

Banana Ricotta Muffins with Blueberries

With the addition of fresh blueberries and ricotta's thick, creamy texture, Banana Ricotta Muffins with Blueberries are a delicious take on traditional banana muffins. These muffins strike a balance between flavours and textures that are both cosy and slightly decadent, making them ideal for breakfast, a snack, or even a light dessert.

There are no better moist and tasty blueberry muffins than Blueberry Ricotta Muffins! This simple muffin recipe with lemon and ricotta cheese will quickly become your new favorite!

You must prepare these muffins if you have any leftover ricotta cheese. They have the nicest crumb and are juicy and fluffy.

You should absolutely start baking using ricotta cheese if you haven't already. Ricotta is a mild-tasting cheese that gives baked goods a rich, moist texture.

These muffins also contain lemon and fresh blueberries in addition to the ricotta. Here, the blueberries and lemons make the ideal mix, with the lemon enhancing the vibrant tastes of the blueberries without overpowering them.

For an Infusion of Freshness, Use Blueberries

Each bite is made brighter by the ideal burst of juiciness and subtle acidity that blueberries contribute. These delicacies are as gorgeous to look at as they are to eat since they not only provide flavor but also create a lovely contrast to the golden-brown muffin. While fresh blueberries are best, frozen blueberries will still work fine; just mix them with a little flour to keep them from sinking.

Ingredients

2 cups (310 grams) of all-purpose flour

1 teaspoon of baking powder

1/2 a teaspoon of baking soda

1/2 tsp kosher salt

1/2 a cup of sugar

½ cup butter, softened

Ricotta cheese, one cup

1 huge egg

1 lemon, juiced and zested (about two tablespoons of juice and ½ teaspoon of zest)

1/2 a cup of blueberries

Instruction

1. Set the oven temperature to 350 degrees. Put liners or cooking spray on a 12-cup muffin tray and set it aside.
2. Mix the flour, baking soda, baking powder, and salt with a whisk and put aside. Beat the sugar, butter, and ricotta in a large basin with a handheld mixer for approximately three minutes, or until light and fluffy. Whisk together the egg, lemon juice, and zest. After adding the dry ingredients, stir the batter until it is barely mixed.
3. The dough will be thick after adding the blueberries, which you may stir in with a rubber spatula.
4. Fill the muffin pans with the batter using a spoon. Put the muffins on the centre rack in the preheated oven and bake for about 23 to 25 minutes, or until a toothpick inserted into the muffin comes out clean. After five minutes of cooling in the pan, move the muffins to a wire rack to finish cooling.

Serving Recommendations

These muffins go nicely with a variety of sides and are quite adaptable. For added sweetness, serve them warm with a drizzle of honey or a dollop of Greek yogurt. A dusting of powdered sugar is a beautiful finishing touch if you're serving them as a breakfast dish or dessert.

Concluding remarks

In addition to being tasty, banana ricotta muffins with blueberries have a cosy, home-cooked feel that makes them perfect for any occasion. They're fancy enough for weekend brunches or sharing with friends, but still easy enough for everyday breakfasts. These muffins are a delicious addition to any recipe collection because they are full of fruit, naturally sweetened, and nutritious.

Chocolate mousse

Rich chocolate taste and a delightfully light, airy texture come together in chocolate mousse, a traditional dessert. You can make a rich confection that tastes and looks opulent yet is incredibly smooth with just a few ingredients and a little perseverance.

The ingredients for mousse are cream and eggs that have been beaten until they are smooth and light. The frothy hair product is also known as mousse because of its texture, which is comparable to these delicacies. Mousse is the Old French word for "froth," but it also denotes, unpleasantly, "scum."

a light, spongy snack that typically contains gelatin or cream. 2. A moulded chilled treat consisting of gelatin chocolate mousse and sweetened and flavoured whipped cream or egg whites. 3. A frothy solution for hair styling.

Unsweetened cocoa powder, water, and a sweetener like sugar can be combined to make a basic chocolate syrup. Other components like malt, corn syrup, and flavourings like vanilla extract may also be called for in recipes.

Why Make Chocolate Mousse?

The key to this dish is balance: it's rich enough to satiate a chocolate need without feeling weighty. It's a sophisticated option for romantic evenings, special events, or merely a decadent treat for oneself. Using the best chocolate you can find makes all the difference since chocolate mousse creates a sophisticated, velvety finish that really showcases the quality of its components.

Ingredients

Three 55g/2 ounce eggs

Dark cooking chocolate, bittersweet, 70% cocoa, 125g/4.5 oz (Note 1)

0.3 ounces (10g) of unsalted butter

1/2 cup full-fat cream (Note 2)

Three tablespoons of caster sugar, or fine white sugar

Instruction

1. Work steadily to avoid overheating your cream and whipped egg whites for consistent results!
2. While the eggs are cool, separate the yolks from the eggs. Put the yolks in a small bowl and the whites in a big bowl. While you prepare the other ingredients, leave the whites alone
3. Yolks: Beat the yolks until they are smooth.
4. Butter and melted chocolate: Break the chocolate into pieces and combine it with the butter in a bowl that can be placed in the microwave. In the microwave, melt in 30-second increments while stirring until smooth. Note 6 should be read before adding optional flavourings. While you continue with the other stages, let it cool slightly.
5. Don't over whip the cream; instead, beat it until stiff peaks form.
6. Beat whites with sugar. Beat the whites until they form stiff peaks.

Fold together all ingredients

Using a rubber spatula, mix the egg yolks into the cream eight times at most. A few streaks are OK.

Verify the chocolate's temperature; it should be warm but still runny (at least 35°C/95°F; at its best, 40°C/104°F). Microwave in 5-second increments until runny if too thick or cool.

Add chocolate to the mixture of cream and yolk. Fold through: no more than eight folds. Here, a few streaks are acceptable.

To the chocolate mixture, add 1/4 of the beaten egg whites. To mix in white lumps, "smear" the spatula across the surface and fold through until integrated; aim for ten folds.

Mix the egg whites with the chocolate mixture. Aim for a maximum of 12 folds, but make sure there are no visible egg whites, and fold through until absorbed and no more white lumps remain.

Distribute the mixture among four tiny pots or glasses. Keep in the fridge for at least six hours, ideally overnight.

Add chocolate shavings and cream as garnish when serving. It would also look great with some raspberries and a small sprig of mint for colour!

Savouring Your Chocolate Mousse

Chocolate mousse melts with every spoonful and has a rich, creamy richness that is best savoured cold. It is suitable for any occasion and goes well with coffee, dessert wines, or effervescent drinks.

The goal of chocolate mousse is to create a delicious moment that may be enjoyed bite by bite. No matter when or where you enjoy it, its elegance produces a lasting impression while its simplicity makes it approachable.